THE BEST OF The MAILBOX® Magazine

Language Arts

GRADES 1–3

Make language arts fun for your students with *The Best Of* The Mailbox® *Language Arts*! This compilation of teaching units—selected from 1988 to 1998 issues of *The Mailbox®* magazine for primary teachers—will energize your language arts lessons and strengthen students' skills. Inside this invaluable classroom resource, you'll find:

- Language arts skill-based units
- Whole-group, small-group, and independent activities
- Literature links
- Reproducibles
- Patterns

D1614257

Editors:
Diane Badden
Amy Erickson

Artists:
Jennifer Tipton Bennett, Cathy Spangler Bruce, Pam Crane,
Nick Greenwood, Clevell Harris, Susan Hodnett, Sheila Krill,
Mary Lester, Rob Mayworth, Kimberly Richard, Rebecca Saunders,
Barry Slate, Donna K. Teal, Irene Maag Wareham

Cover Artist:
Jennifer Tipton Bennett

Table Of Contents

©1998 by THE EDUCATION CENTER, INC.
All rights reserved.
ISBN #1-56234-258-4

Manufactured in the United States
10 9 8 7 6 5 4 3 2 1

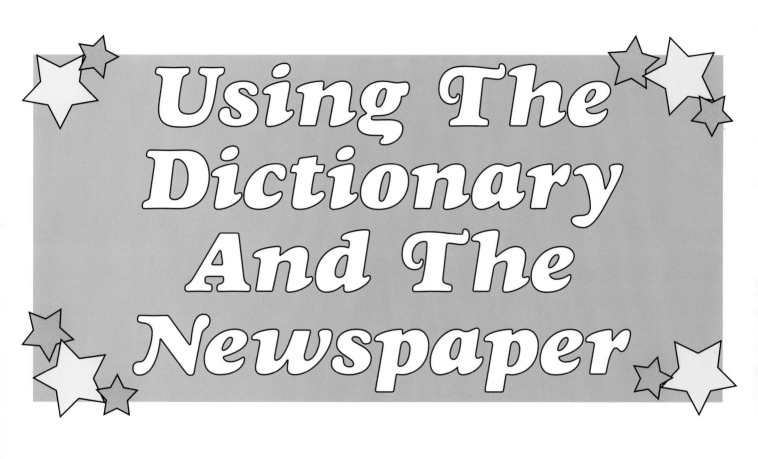

Using The Dictionary And The Newspaper

Hot Diggity—Dictionaries!

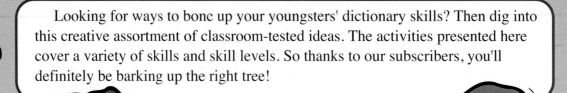

Looking for ways to bone up your youngsters' dictionary skills? Then dig into this creative assortment of classroom-tested ideas. The activities presented here cover a variety of skills and skill levels. So thanks to our subscribers, you'll definitely be barking up the right tree!

Dictionary Readiness

Here's a fun way for youngsters to learn the beginning, middle, and ending letters of the alphabet. Each student needs a spiral notebook. Sequentially program the pages of each notebook with the letters of the alphabet, allowing two pages per letter. Every morning write a mystery word on the chalkboard in number code (A = 1, B = 2, C = 3, etc.). Students decode the word and write it in their spiral "dictionaries." If desired, have students write the word in a sentence after its meaning has been discussed.

Karen Saner—Gr. 1, Burns Elementary School, Burns, KS

I Used The Dictionary!

Turn using the dictionary into a big deal with this reward system. Each time a student looks up a word in the dictionary, have him write the word and the corresponding dictionary page number on a laminated poster titled "I Used The Dictionary!" At the end of the day, place one marble in a reward jar for each word listed on the poster. When the jar is completely filled, reward your youngsters with a special class privilege.

Shirley Gillette—Chapter I Reading, Lafe Nelson School Safford, AZ

A Few Of Our Favorite Things

A is for applesauce, *B* is for balloons, *C* is for chocolate. Here's a great way for youngsters to get acquainted with the dictionary! For each child, staple 26 blank pages between two slightly larger construction-paper covers. Next have each youngster label his pages in alphabetical order. Then, using a dictionary for guidance, have each child label and illustrate one favorite item per page. Z is for zest...while using the dictionary!

Ann Lynch—Gr. 1
Quarry Hill Community School
Monson, MA

Alphabet Notebooks

Familiarize your youngsters with the dictionary by having each student keep a yearlong alphabet notebook. At the beginning of the school year, present each youngster with a spiral notebook. (In advance sequentially alphabetize the pages and personalize the cover of each child's "dictionary.") For the first activity, have each child list his name on the appropriate page in his notebook. Then, throughout the year, encourage youngsters to enter a variety of words such as number words, color words, holiday words, vocabulary words, and science words. Also suggest that youngsters refer to their notebooks when they are writing stories. At the end of the year, your students' notebooks will be bursting with words and your students will be bursting with pride!

Wendy Wootten—Gr. 1, Westside Primary School Quantico, MD

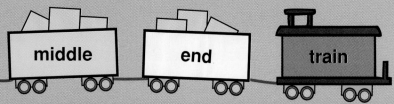

The Alphabet Express

Everyone knows that a train has a beginning, a middle, and an end; so why should a dictionary train be any different? To make this sorting center, label train cutouts as shown. If desired, staple the cutouts to a bulletin board, making certain that a pocket is formed behind each train car. Provide an assortment of word cards. A student sorts each card into the appropriate train car. If desired program the backs of the word cards for self-checking. Choo! Choo!

Shirley Kennon—Gr. 2, San Antonio, TX

A Classy Dictionary

This project results in a very unique picture dictionary! To begin have each youngster draw a self-portrait on a two-inch square of white paper. Next have him attach his drawing to the lower right-hand corner of a 4 1/2" x 8" sheet of writing paper. On the top line of his paper, have each youngster use a crayon or marker to write his last name first, followed by his first name. Then in pencil, have each child write five sentences that describe himself, numbering each sentence. Enlist the help of students in sequencing their completed dictionary entries. Mount the entries in pairs on 9" x 12" sheets of construction paper. Add a title page and a desired cover. Before binding the project together, duplicate student copies of the completed project. Now that's a dictionary keepsake!

Sr. Julie Gatza—Gr. 3, St. James School, Bay City, MI

Matchmakers

At this center, students use a dictionary to match unusual words to their meanings. Program a desired number of index cards with unusual words (one word per card). Then, for each word card, program an index card with its meaning. Sort the cards into sets (for example: four word cards and their matching definition cards); then place each set in a resealable plastic bag. Number the resulting activity packets for easy identification. Place the packets at a center. To help students keep track of the packets they complete, give each student a duplicated management chart. Each day a student completes one packet. After his work has been approved, the appropriate section of his chart is initialed by the teacher.

Loni Baker—Gr. 2
Lancaster Elementary School
Bluffton, IN

Word-A-Day Homework

Enhance youngsters' vocabularies and dictionary skills with this daily homework assignment. Each day have youngsters copy a designated word from the chalkboard into their word-a-day notebooks. If desired, relate the word to a current study theme such as plants, careers, or mammals. That evening the student finds the word in his family's dictionary and copies the corresponding definition in his notebook. (In a parent letter, explain this activity and encourage parents to initially provide assistance using the dictionary as needed.) The following morning have students share the information that they found. At the end of each thematic study unit, present students with awards of recognition stating the number of thematic words that they have investigated.

Renee Larsen—Gr. 2, Adams School, Fergus Falls, MN

Early Arrivals

Challenge your early arrivals with a daily list of mystery words. Display a list of three or four words on the chalkboard each morning. Students who arrive early can find the words in their dictionaries. After everyone has settled in, ask volunteer students to share the meanings of the day's words.

Pat Wight—Gr. 3, Friday Harbor Elementary School, Friday Harbor, WA

words
quiver
dewlap
cupola
palisade

meanings
a case for holding arrows
a loose fold of skin hanging under the neck of certain animals
a rounded roof
a line of high cliffs

Just The Beginning...

To begin this dictionary project, assign each child a different alphabet letter. (If you have more than 26 children, some letters will be assigned more than once.) Next have each student choose a word from a picture dictionary that begins with his assigned letter, then write and illustrate his chosen word on a 9" x 12" sheet of construction paper. Sequentially compile the completed pages in a large three-ring binder. Throughout the school year, encourage youngsters to create additional pages for their class dictionary. By the end of the year, the dictionary will be chock-full of personalized pages!

Mary Rubino Kibbey—Gr. 1, Athens Elementary, Earlton, NY

An Open-And-Shut Case

Each student needs a dictionary for this small group activity. After calling out a word, challenge each student in the group to try to open his dictionary to the exact page where the word can be found. If desired award points as follows: 10 points = the exact page, 5 points = the correct letter of the alphabet, 1 point = the correct section of the dictionary. Kids love the activity, and it helps them become more efficient at looking up words.

Tammie Boone, Sheldon, IA

Seasonal Riddles

What's in the pond? Your youngsters will be eager to find out! For an end-of-the-year dictionary activity, decorate a bulletin board to resemble a pond in summer. Each day mount a riddle in the middle of the pond. For example: "I float on the pond. I might have a flower when you see me. What am I?" Have each youngster submit his answer on a personalized paper slip. Encourage each student to verify his answer in a dictionary by checking the meaning and the spelling of the word that he submits. At the end of the day, give a sticker or other small prize to each student who submitted a correct (and correctly spelled) answer. This activity can easily be adapted to other seasonal topics. For example: "What's In the Pumpkin?", "What's In Santa's Bag?", and "What's In the Snowman's Hat?"

Frieda Oelrich—Gr. 1, Spencer Elementary School, Spencer, WI

Hot Off The Press

At the completion of this activity, each student will have created a thematic dictionary page. Equip a center with a typewriter, typing paper, a dictionary, and a word list related to a topic that your youngsters will soon be studying. Then, using a page from the dictionary as a guide, each student sets up his dictionary page by typing two guide words and five or more entry words from the provided list. For a bit of fun, have students create definitions for their entry words without the help of the dictionary. Collect the projects; then near the completion of your thematic study, return the dictionary pages and invite students to compare their definitions with the correct meanings of the words. Be prepared for a gaggle of giggles!

Teresia C. Matrafailo—Gr. 2, Pakanasink Elementary School Circleville, NY

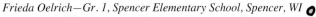

Sentence Stumpers

Hook your youngsters on using the dictionary with this simple sentence activity. Each morning write a sentence on the chalkboard that contains an unfamiliar word. For example: The men rode across the water on a *sampan*. Without a doubt your youngsters will be scouring their dictionaries to discover the meaning of the new word.

Sharee Wilkerson—Gr. 2
South Knoll Elementary
College Station, TX

Digging Into The Dictionary

If you're looking for a dictionary activity that's easy to program and easy to grade, consider the student activity on page 164. To use this reproducible, simply program a copy of the original with a desired entry word and sample sentence. For easy grading, assign a 20-point value to each of the five possible answers. When accountability is a must, reach for this activity.

Dale Hegler—Gr. 2
Sullivan's Island Elementary
Sullivan's Island, SC

Dictionary!

This game provides practice in quickly opening a dictionary to the appropriate section. Before each round of play, have students position their dictionaries atop their desks in starting positions: book spines resting atop the desks, covers parallel. Next write a selected word on the chalkboard, beginning with the last letter. Students may begin searching for the word as soon as the chalk is laid down. The first student to find the word calls out, "Dictionary!" All students stop immediately and listen for the appropriate page number, guide words, and definition. If the child is correct, he earns a sticker and all players return their dictionaries to starting positions. If the child is incorrect, the round resumes until a correct response is given.

Audra Borowski—Gr. 3, Thomas Fitzwater Elementary
Willow Grove, PA

The Dictionary Depot

Try this class activity to familiarize your youngsters with the dictionary. To prepare for the activity, have students write unfamiliar words from their reading on individual word cards. Ask students to deposit the cards in a decorated container labeled "The Dictionary Depot." Each day, choose one card from the container and have students find the word in their dictionaries. As a class, discuss the meaning, the spelling, and the pronunciation of the word; then talk about the dictionary page where the word was found. Next ask a volunteer student to copy the meaning of the word on the card before displaying the card at a class word bank. When approximately 20 new words have been learned, use the words and their definitions to play a game of Bingo.

Debbie Grecco—Gr. 3, Northwest Elementary School, Butler, PA

Pictionary Dictionary

Try this fun approach to dictionary practice. Divide students into two teams. Each student needs a dictionary. To begin play, have one player from each team advance to the chalkboard. Secretly show both players the same entry word. On "Go," both players begin drawing picture clues about the word on the chalkboard. Each seated player quickly finds his word guess in his dictionary and raises his hand. The first student to read the appropriate word and its meaning from his dictionary earns one point for his team. Play continues until each student has taken a turn at the chalkboard. The team with the most points wins.

Paige Brannon—Gr. 3, Pitt County Schools, Greenville, NC

Find It Fast!

Reinforce dictionary skills by playing this fast-paced relay game. Divide students into four equal teams. Have the members of each team sit single file by aligning their chairs one behind the other. Give the first member of each team a dictionary, a pencil, and a large index card labeled with a word list (one word per team player). The words on each team card should be the same; however, the order of the words may vary. On "Go," the first member of each team finds the first word in his dictionary; then on the card, beside the word, he writes the corresponding dictionary page number and guide words. He then passes the word card, dictionary, and pencil to his teammate sitting directly behind him. Play continues in this manner until each team has completed its card. A team earns ten points for a correctly completed card. Award an additional five points to the team that correctly completed its card first. Before beginning another round of play, have the last student on each team move his chair to the front of his team. Continue play until all students have completed a round of play in each playing position or until time runs out. The team with the most points wins.

Gina Brooks—Gr. 3, Deerfield Elementary School, Short Hills, NJ

1. craft   p.131 cracker/crawl
2. motor   p. 382 mostly/motor
3. silent   p. 545 Germany/ghost
1. melon   p. 255 m
2. valve   p. 849 value/vamoose

Name _____

Digging Into The Dictionary

Carefully read the entry word and the sample sentence.

Entry word: _____

Sample sentence: _____

_____

_____

_____

Find the entry word in a dictionary.
Answer the questions.

1. What is the name of the dictionary that you are using? _____

_____

2. On what dictionary page did you find the entry word? _____

3. What are the two guide words on this page?

_____   _____

4. What does the entry word mean in the sample sentence above?
   (Copy the matching definition from the dictionary.)

_____

_____

Write the entry word in a sentence of your own.
Underline the entry word.

_____

_____

Note To Teacher: See "Digging Into The Dictionary" on page 6 for how to use this sheet.

Hot Off The Press!

Utilizing The Newspaper In The Classroom

Extra! Extra! Read all about it! Here's the inside scoop on using the newspaper in the classroom. We've gathered newsworthy tips and activities from a most reliable and respected source—our trusty subscribers—and we've published the best of the batch in this news-breaking collection. You can count on us to deliver!

Easy Does It

The format of newspapers makes them difficult for students to handle. To keep the oversized pages from slipping and sliding, place several staples down the left-hand edge of each newspaper.

Dee Ann Bates
Hawthorne Elementary
Oklahoma City, OK

Not Just For Grown–Ups!

Beginning readers often think that the newspaper is just for adults. Use this activity to convince your youngsters that they can read the newspaper, too! Have each student choose a different newspaper article and circle each word in the article that he can read. Then ask each student to count the number of circled words and write that number near the top of the article. By gum, students can read the newspaper!

Sally Bivins—Gr. 1, Apache Elementary School, Peoria, AZ

Front–Page News

Get the scoop on front-page news! Enlist your youngsters' help in comparing and contrasting a similar news story from two different newspapers. Read aloud the two articles; then as a class create a large Venn diagram that shows the similarities and differences between the two stories. This activity also works well with sports coverage and movie reviews.

Kelly Pflederer—Gr. 2, Academy Of The Sacred Heart, St. Louis, MO

Pam Crane

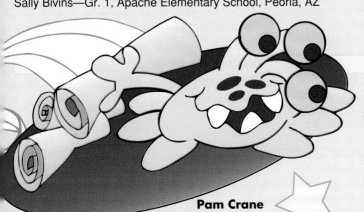

Comic Capers

This large-group sequencing activity leaves youngsters smiling from ear to ear! To prepare for the fun, each student cuts out her favorite comic strip from a discarded newspaper. She cuts apart the individual frames and mounts each one on a construction-paper rectangle; then she sequences the mounted frames and programs the backs for self-checking. Next she writes her name and the name of her comic strip on a library pocket before she randomly slips the pieces of her project inside. To begin the large-group activity, each student places her project on her desktop. The students then move from desk to desk along a prearranged route and work the projects their classmates have prepared. There'll be plenty of reading, sequencing, and chuckling taking place!

Marcia Dosser—Gr. 1
Eastern Tennessee State University School, Johnson City, TN

Attention–Grabbing Advertisements

Students may be surprised to discover the number of advertisements found in a newspaper. Display a few newspaper pages; then use a colored marker to circle the ads featured. As a class, critique the advertisements. Discuss what makes an effective ad and why the newspaper is a good medium for advertisers. Then challenge each child to create an attention-grabbing newspaper advertisement for a brand-new product or service. Set aside time for students to share their creative work; then showcase the ads around the school!

Lilly Schultz—Resource Teacher, Washington Elementary School, Auburn, WA

Movie Madness

Interpreting a movie schedule is a picture-perfect way for students to practice reading and interpreting information. Give each group or individual a similar movie listing from the newspaper. Pose a series of questions that require the students to interpret the information at hand. Be sure to include some problem-solving challenges as well!

Lilly Schultz—Resource Teacher

News And Views

Reinforce comprehension, critical thinking, and writing skills with this newsworthy idea. Each week bring to school a different newspaper article that you feel will be of special interest to your youngsters. Read the article aloud; then discuss it as a class. Pose several questions that require students to think critically about the information presented. In conclusion have each child write a paragraph that describes and defends his opinion about the news topic. Mount the completed paragraphs along with the featured news article on a bulletin board titled "News And Views."

Laura Horowitz—Gr. 2
Plantation, FL

Pulverized

Action Packed!

If you're looking for verbs, try the sports page—it's packed with action! Challenge students to find a predetermined number of past, present, and/or future-tense verbs on their newspaper pages. Or have students find ten past-tense verbs in the newspaper, then write the present and future tenses of the verbs on their papers. You'll have plenty of verbs and plenty of possibilities for skill reinforcement!

Pam Williams, Lakeland, FL

Autos For Sale

Shopping for cars is a unique way to provide students with practice in reading large numbers. Each student needs a newspaper page that lists automobiles for sale. Youngsters can choose the cars they'd like to buy and read aloud the corresponding prices. Or ask each student to read aloud the highest (lowest) priced car on his page. Sequencing car prices is also an excellent way to reinforce place-value skills. Vroom! Math practice is picking up speed!

Pam Williams

TURBO SPACE CRUISER for sale. Like-new condition. **CHEAP.** $12,090.00

Graphing The Weather

Tracking the weather offers lots of learning opportunities. For a weeklong graphing activity, have students graph the daily high and low temperatures of cities across the country. To do this a student chooses a city that appears daily in the local paper's weather column and records the information on a duplicated graph. At the end of the week, students can report their cities' high and low temperatures for that week. The class can then determine which city had the highest (lowest) temperature of the week and find the corresponding cities on an appropriate map. Students can also graph and tally precipitation readings. Who knows? Youngsters may even like to test their talents at making weather predictions!

Theodora Gallagher—Gr. 1, Carteret School, Bloomfield, NJ

Newspaper Portfolios

These nifty (and newsy!) carryalls are perfect for storing or transporting newspaper projects. To make a portfolio that holds 9" x 12" projects, stack and align two full-size sheets of newspaper. Position the papers so that the center crease runs horizontally across the papers. Create a three-inch fold along the right and left edges of the project and along the bottom of the project as shown. Keep these folds in place as you bring the bottom of the project upward and make a fold along the crease line. Staple along each side. Fold down the top of the project to create a flap. Crease this fold; then unfold the flap and punch two holes near the center of the resulting crease— about four inches apart. For added durability, attach lengths of tape to both sides of each hole and repunch the holes. To make a sturdy handle, repeatedly thread a length of yarn through the holes; then securely tie the yarn ends. Refold the flap and your portfolio is ready to use!

Theodora Gallagher—Gr. 1

Comic Booklets

Use the Sunday comics to turn a parts-of-speech review into a barrel of laughs! To make a comic booklet, label a 6" x 9" rectangle of construction paper for each part of speech to be reviewed. Staple the resulting pages between construction-paper covers. For each booklet page, find one comic-strip frame that has a written example of the featured part of speech. Use a crayon to underline the example; then cut out the frame and mount it on the appropriate booklet page. To complete each page, write a brief definition of the spotlighted part of speech. Add a title and byline to the booklet cover, and this newspaper project is complete!

Susan M. Stires—Gr. 3, Alamo Elementary School, Wichita Falls, TX

Tracking Down Numbers

Energize a math review with a number search! Each youngster needs crayons and a few newspaper pages. Challenge students to find numerals based on certain criteria. Directions could include, "Use a red crayon to circle a three-digit numeral that has a six in the tens place," and "Draw a green box around a numeral that is greater than 75." Provide a greater challenge with directions like, "Find two numbers whose sum equals ten. Draw a yellow star on each number." The possibilities are endless! Be sure students understand that this activity includes an element of chance like the game of bingo. This will prevent students from feeling frustrated if they cannot find all the numbers.

Kelly Malandra—Gr. 3, Lorane Elementary School, Exeter Township, PA

Making Comparisons

Comparing newspapers from different communities provides a wealth of learning opportunities. As a class choose several communities from which you'd like to obtain newspapers. Divide the class into small groups; then ask each group to compose a letter that requests a sample newspaper and offers to pay for the requested newspaper and mailing costs. Mail the letters to the communities on your class list. (Most libraries have a reference, such as *Editor & Publisher International Year Book* or *Gale Directory Of Publications And Broadcast Media,* that lists the names and mailing addresses of newspapers.) When each paper arrives, compare and contrast its news coverage with that of your local paper for the same day. Students will enjoy comparing the comics, the weather, and the movie selections, too. Be sure to send a thank-you note to each newspaper that participates in your project.

Pam Doerr—Substitute Teacher, Elizabethtown District, Elizabethtown, PA

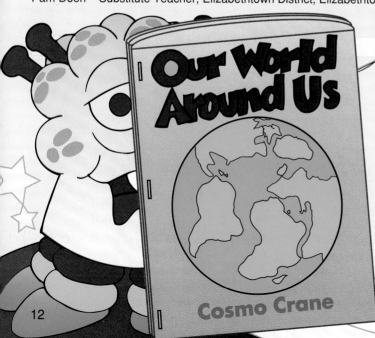

A Continental Study

Learning the continents of the world is in the bag with this individual booklet project. To make a booklet, stack eight flat paper bags; then staple the bags together along the left-hand edge. Personalize, attach a cutout of the world, and write the title "Our World Around Us" on the top bag. On each of the following bags, attach and label a cutout of a different continent. To complete his booklet, a student cuts out newspaper articles and determines where each news event took place. Then he slips each article into the appropriate continent bag. Encourage youngsters to find five or more articles per continent.

Patti A. Devall—Gr. 3, St. Anthony Grade School, Effingham, IL

As Easy As ABC!

Searching for a quick-and-easy review of alphabetical order? Look no further than the daily news. Ask each student to cut out ten or more words from a newspaper, then glue the words on his paper in ABC order. For a more challenging activity, ask students to cut out words that represent an assigned theme (like weather, sports, or music) or a category (like verbs, adjectives, or nouns).

Pam Negovetich—Gr. 3, Ready Elementary, Griffith, IN

What A Great Photo!

Get a little help from the newspaper for a great sentence-writing activity. Ask each youngster to find a newspaper photo that she really likes, then cut it out and mount it on construction paper. For a writing assignment, challenge each student to write a question, a statement, a command, and an exclamatory sentence about her picture. The students are writing about topics they enjoy—and when the activity is completed, you'll have a clear indication of each student's sentence-writing capabilities. Later showcase the mounted pictures at a creative-writing center. You'll have a gallery of writing inspiration!

Pam Negovetich—Gr. 3

Graph It!

This class graphing activity is full of laughs! Cut out the comic strips featured in your local newspaper. Count the strips you have; then divide the class into an equal number of groups. Give each group one comic strip and ask the group to count the words shown on its strip. Enlist your students' help in graphing the results on a class graph and in interpreting the information presented. If desired, repeat the activity for several days using current comic strips each time. Students will enjoy comparing and contrasting the data, and making predictions about the comic strips for the following day, such as, "I predict that Garfield will have the least number of words."

Susan Barnett—Gr. 3, Northwest Elementary School
Fort Wayne, IN

Shop 'Til You Drop!

For this activity choose a local grocery store's advertising supplement from your newspaper and use it to create a shopping list. If you're designing a center activity, you'll need only one supplement. If you're planning to have your youngsters complete the activity simultaneously, you'll need one supplement for every one or two students. (Enlist your youngsters' help in gathering the supplements, or ask a local grocer for additional copies.) Display the shopping list and challenge each student to use his advertising supplement to determine the total cost of the items. Include a list of discount coupons that the students may apply to their purchases, if desired. Depending on the nature of the shopping list, a variety of math skills can be reinforced. Students are also learning important consumer concepts. Shop on!

Shannon Tovey—Gr. 3, George Peabody Elementary School, Dallas, TX

Understanding Headlines

So what's in a headline? Challenge students to find out! Read aloud a newspaper headline and ask students to predict what the corresponding article will be about. When all of the predictions are in, read the article aloud or give a brief summary of it. Then reexamine the headline and determine what the key words are. Repeat the activity several times. For a fun twist, read aloud a newspaper article and challenge students to write an appropriate headline!

Tammy Brinkman & Kimberly Martin—Gr. 3
Dellview Elementary
San Antonio, TX

Zorkian Caught In Sticky Situation?!?!

Making Use Of Maps

The newspaper is an excellent resource for maps—from local city maps to maps of the world. To take advantage of this offering, create a special file for newspaper maps. Each time a unique map is featured, clip it out and file it for later use. Most of the maps are easy to enlarge or duplicate. Or you can laminate the maps for individual student use. You'll soon wonder how you ever got along without this excellent resource.

Tammy Brinkman & Kimberly Martin—Gr. 3

Mugging It Up

This activity is a sight to see! Ask each student to bring to school a coffee mug. Personalize the bottom of the mugs; then display the mug collection on cup hooks or store it in a classroom cupboard. One morning a week, use the mugs to serve a desired beverage; then distribute a newspaper page to each child. On the chalkboard list several items for the students to find in their newspapers, such as two nouns, a contraction, a compound word, three plurals, and an action verb. As students sip their beverages, they read their papers and use crayons to circle the requested items. The students feel quite grown-up as they enjoy the daily news!

Ginger Becker—Gr. 2
Marion Elementary School
Marion, KS

Happily Ever After

For one-of-a-kind writing inspiration, check the Lost & Found listing in the classified ads. Cut apart and store the individual listings in a container. When you have a student supply, have each child draw a listing from the container and glue it to the top of his story paper. Then have each child write and illustrate a story that describes how a family pet is reunited with its family or how a family becomes the proud owner of a stranded pet.

Terry Kelly—Gr. 3, Prospect Elementary, East Cleveland, OH

Basic Reading Skills

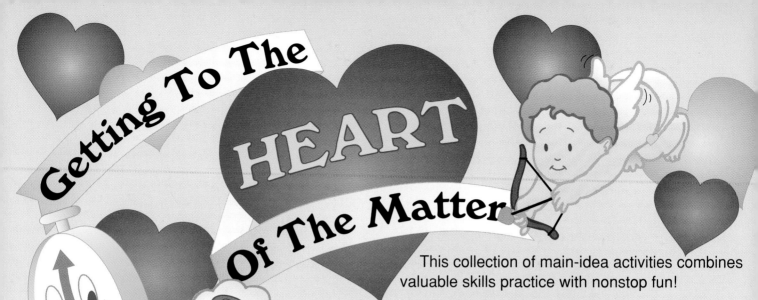

Getting To The HEART Of The Matter

This collection of main-idea activities combines valuable skills practice with nonstop fun!

Refreshing Riddles

This main-idea activity fills your classroom with giggles galore! Read several riddles to your children from a riddle book. Allow students to answer the riddles and to explain how they determined the answers. Then allow them to work individually or in groups to create their own riddles. Have students share their riddles with one another. Then explain to students that the clues in a riddle are the *details* and that the answer is the *main idea*. Conclude the activity by identifying the details and the main idea of each child's riddle.

What has a face and two hands but no body?

Lana Stewart—Gr. 2, Haskell Elementary, Haskell, TX

Main-Idea Hamburger

Have fun teaching the main idea of paragraphs with this mouth-watering demonstration. On a sheet of chart paper, draw a large hamburger. While explaining the parts of a paragraph, label the hamburger as follows:
— top bun: introduction
— meat: main idea
— lettuce, tomato, pickles: details
— bottom bun: conclusion
Provide practice by reading a paragraph to your youngsters. Then have students identify the parts of the paragraph as you record their responses on another hamburger drawing.

Lisa Conway—Gr. 2, John J. Daly School, Port Washington, NY

introduction
main idea
detail
detail
detail
conclusion

Handy Practice

This personalized activity gives students a handful of practice. Have each child trace his hand on a sheet of construction paper. Then have him cut out the resulting outline. Have the child use a marker to write his name on the palm of the hand cutout. On each finger of the cutout, have the child write a detail about himself. Explain to students that their names tell the main idea and that the bits of information on the fingers are the details. Mount students' completed cutouts on a bulletin board titled "We've Got The Main Idea Hands Down!"

Patrice Cassidy—Grs. 1-5 Resource
Settlers Way Elementary
Sugar Land, TX

Teasers

This activity heightens students' reading interest as it lends itself to a variety of main-idea activities. To begin, display several books for your students. Have them locate the information on the back of each paperback book and on the jacket of each hardcover book. Explain that this information, called the *teaser,* tells the main idea of the book and tries to entice someone to read the book. Read several teasers to your children and then discuss why they are called teasers. In the future, develop a routine of reading each book's teaser before beginning the story. For more fun with teasers, try the activities below.

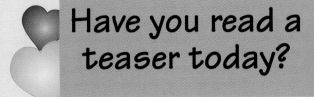

1. Read a book to your students without reading the teaser ahead of time. Then change the teaser by adding an element that does not belong. Read aloud the changed version of the teaser and have students identify the element that was not a part of the story.

2. Fill your spare moments with Teaser Time. During this time, read the teaser of a familiar story to your youngsters without identifying the book's title. Then have students name the book.

3. Read a story to your children. Then, as a class, write a teaser to accompany the book. Extend this activity by having children work individually or in cooperative groups to compose teasers for different books.

Joanne Rosengren, Nashotah, WI

Picture This!

Get ready for fun! This activity uses visual aids for your students' main-idea practice. Divide your students into groups of three or four. Then give each group a picture (cut from a discarded magazine) that depicts an event or an interesting situation. Have each group discuss its picture and tell the main idea. Have the groups rotate their pictures for added practice.

Donna Gregory—Grs. 1-2
Hodge Elementary
Denton, TX

Main-Idea Quilts

These brightly colored paper quilts help students demonstrate their understanding of the main-idea concept. Read a short story to your class. Then have each child cut out a background for her quilt from a sheet of 9" x 12" construction paper. Next have each child cut out five or six circle or square shapes from different colors of construction paper. On one of the shapes, have the child use a marker to write the main idea. Then have her glue the shape to the center of her quilt background. On each of the remaining shapes, the child writes a story detail to support the main idea. Then she glues her detail shapes around the main idea. Have each child complete her main-idea quilt by adding designs, outlines, and stitch marks using colored markers.

Jeannette Freeman—Gr. 3
Baldwin School Of Puerto Rico
Guaynabo, PR

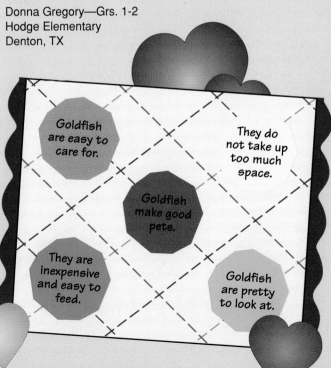

The Gist Of Journal Writing

Here's a great way for students to identify the main ideas of their classmates' writing. After your daily journal-writing sessions, allow students to share their entries with their classmates. Then have them determine the main idea of each child's entry. This activity not only provides practice in identifying the main idea, but also encourages students to express themselves clearly in writing.

Tami Fedor—Gr. 1, Lenoir City Elementary, Lenoir City, TN

Main-Event Newsletter

Inform parents of your weekly classroom events with this thought-provoking activity. At the end of each day, have students reflect on their daily activities and determine the main idea of each of their lessons. As students dictate sentences to you, record their responses on chart paper. At the end of the week, transfer these main-idea sentences onto a newsletter to duplicate and send home.

Tami Fedor—Gr. 1

A Year Full Of Main-Idea Practice

Practice finding main ideas throughout the year with an array of monthly literature-based art projects. At the beginning of each month, duplicate a seasonal shape for each child. For example, in February duplicate a pattern of a heart-shaped candy box. Each day read a chapter of a book to students. Then have each student glue a candy cut-out illustrated with the chapter's main idea to his candy box. Continue in this manner each day until the story is complete. Each child's resulting project is a visual summary of the book. Adapt this activity for use throughout the school year by assembling projects such as turkeys in November, candy-filled stockings in December, and flower-filled baskets in May.

Maria Mathiesen and Amy Fox—Gr. 2
Notre Dame Elementary
East Stroudsburg, PA

Horrible Harry In Room 2B

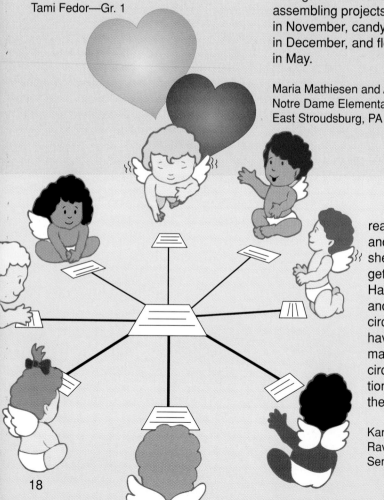

Spider "Main-ia"

Students create a web of details with this fun activity. After reading a story to your children, give each child an index card and a length of yarn. On her card, have each child write a detail she remembers from the story. Then have all students sit together in a circle with their cards positioned in front of them. Have each child place one end of her yarn on her index card and extend the opposite end of the yarn toward the center of the circle. Have each child share her story detail with the class; then have the class determine the main idea of the story. Write the main idea on an index card and place it in the center of the circle, connecting it to the lengths of yarn. Draw students' attention to the fact that the details of a story support and connect to the main idea.

Karen Walden—Gr. 1
Ravenel Elementary
Seneca, SC

Chapter Titles

While reading a chapter book to your students, take a few minutes each day to discuss the title of the chapter you'll be reading. Ask students to discuss what they think will happen in the chapter based on its title. After reading the chapter to your children, have them discuss the events and decide if the chapter needs a more appropriate title. At the end of the book, have students reflect on the events of the story and create a new title for the entire book. Ask students to explain their reasons for choosing the new title.

Some books use numbers rather than titles for the chapters. When reading this kind of book, have students discuss the events of each chapter and then create a title based on these details. Write the titles on sticky notes and attach them to the appropriate pages of the book.

Joanne Rosengren, Nashotah, WI

Playing in the snow is fun.

Dad is a hard worker.

Cleaning my room is a lot of work.

Sentence Speculation

This is a job for the main-idea detectives! On each of several legal-sized envelopes, write a main-idea sentence. Display the envelopes along your chalkboard tray. Then, for each main idea, label each of several index cards with a detail sentence. Distribute the cards randomly among your students. Have students place their detail cards in the corresponding main-idea envelopes. After all cards have been placed, read the contents of each envelope. Allow students to determine whether or not each detail supports the main idea. Extend this activity by writing each group of sentences on a sheet of chart paper to form a paragraph.

Andrea Masone
Houston, TX

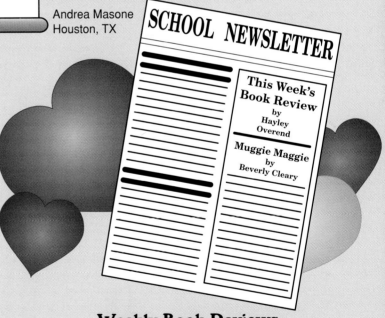

Book Talks

Model main-idea skills daily by engaging in book talks. In order to pique students' reading interest and to demonstrate these skills, summarize a book for your students each day. Then periodically assign each child a time to give a book talk to his classmates. You'll notice your students' main-idea skills improving as they become more experienced with giving book talks.

Janiel Wagstaff—Gr. 2, Bennion Elementary, Salt Lake City, UT

Weekly Book Reviews

Students become book critics with this fun routine. Each week assign one student to write a book review including a book's main idea and several supporting details. Copy an edited version of this review onto your weekly parent newsletter. Parents will delight in these intriguing accounts of their children's reading experiences.

Janiel Wagstaff—Gr. 2

WORD WATCHERS!

Double Draw

This booklet activity is highly adaptable and can be used for any subject, season, or holiday that has its own specialized vocabulary. Choose a topic and write vocabulary words related to the topic on individual slips of paper (one per student). Place the programmed papers in a decorated container, and give each youngster a booklet page of the desired size and shape. A student draws a vocabulary word from the container and writes it near the top of his paper. Next he writes the word in a complete sentence and illustrates it. After each child has shared his completed booklet page, staple the pages in alphabetical order between a decorated cover. Keep these booklets on display in your classroom library.

Word Collages

Make use of discarded magazines and newspapers as you increase your students' word awareness. To make a word collage, a student looks through several discarded newspapers and/or magazines. Each time he finds a word that he thinks is interesting, he cuts it out. When he has a supply of word cutouts, he randomly glues them on a 12" x 18" sheet of construction paper. Encourage students to look for words of different sizes and colors, words that are written in unusual type styles, and words of various lengths. Once the collages are completed, have students discuss their projects with partners and find unfamiliar words in their dictionaries. Then as a class activity, have each youngster name and describe a favorite word from his collage. Display the completed projects on a bulletin board for all to enjoy.

Object Of The Day

As a part of your morning routine, display an object of the day. On the chalkboard write five words that describe the object. Elicit four of the words from your youngsters. Provide the fifth word yourself, attempting to list a word that is unfamiliar to most students. Use these five words throughout the day in your lessons and conversations, and encourage your students to do the same. By the end of the day, most youngsters will have familiarized themselves with at least one new vocabulary word. Enlist your students' help in providing objects for this activity.

Word Of The Day

This activity gives each student the opportunity to teach an interesting vocabulary word to his classmates. In a letter sent home, ask parents to assist their children in selecting interesting vocabulary words. Explain that each youngster must be able to say and write his vocabulary word and explain its meaning. Suggest that parents look for interesting words in the news media, in their vocations, and on product labels.

Ideas For Vocabulary Expansion

Words! Words! Words! Increase your youngsters' writing, speaking, listening, and reading vocabularies with these motivational activities and reproducibles.

ideas contributed by Joyce Swan

Character Studies

Increase your youngsters' descriptive vocabularies by taking a closer look at the characters featured in your current read-aloud. For each character, draw a simple chart like the one shown. On the left side of the chart, list the character's actions as described in the story. On the right side of the chart, list other words that describe these actions. Older students can complete this activity independently using the books they are currently reading.

Charlie	
Things that Charlie did:	Other words to describe these actions:
did not spend money	stingy, tight, greedy
saved a friend's life	courageous, brave, clever

The Word Corner

For a fun free-time center, set up a Word Corner. At the center place a collection of games such as Scrabble, Boggle, and Spill And Spell. Also keep several dictionaries at the center and encourage students to use them as they play the games. Add to your collection of word games throughout the year. Check yard sales for good buys on used games for the center.

Creative Vocabulary

Here's an activity your youngsters are sure to love. Make a list of unusual words that are unknown to most students. Periodically choose one word from the list and write (and underline) the word in a sentence on the board. Instruct students to read the sentence carefully as they try to derive the meaning of the underlined word. Then have each student draw and color a picture that shows what he thinks the word means. Encourage students to share their illustrations. Be sure to praise students for their creative thinking. Then conclude the activity by finding the correct meaning of the word in a dictionary. Here are a few sentences to get you started:

1. The old man was wearing a black <u>fedora</u>. *(a felt hat)*
2. Mary proudly wore her new <u>cerise</u> coat. *(red)*
3. The teacher scolded the <u>loquacious</u> students. *(talkative)*
4. No one liked the <u>stingy</u> king. *(unwilling to share)*
5. The beautiful <u>cob</u> swam slowly. *(a male swan)*

Fun With Words Through Literature

At the mere mention of Amelia Bedelia (the main character in a series of books authored by Peggy Parish), you'll probably hear squeals of delight from your students. Amelia's literal interpretations of words land her in some of the most outrageous situations. Discussing and predicting Amelia's antics are great ways to enrich students' vocabularies. Another fun book of a similar nature is *The King Who Rained* by Fred Gwynne. In this delightful book, a young child visualizes what her parents tell in funny (literal) ways. Ask your media specialist for assistance in finding these and other books of this type.

Ruth Heller has also written a collection of colorful and rhythmic books that are superb for extending language. *A Cache Of Jewels & Other Collective Nouns*, *Many Luscious Lollipops: A Book About Adjectives*, *Kites Sail High: A Book About Verbs*, and *Merry-Go-Round: A Book About Nouns* are filled with endless language opportunities.

TRDavidson

Daily Vocabulary Builder

Increase your students' vocabularies with this daily activity. For each student, staple 26 blank pages between two slightly larger construction-paper covers. Then have each youngster label his booklet pages in alphabetical order. As a homework activity, give each student an index card and instruct him to cut an interesting word from a discarded item in his home (such as a magazine, newspaper, or cereal box) and attach the cutout to the card. Have students deposit their completed cards in a decorated container labeled "The Discovery Box." Each day, one student draws a card from the box. This student is responsible for discovering the meaning of the word he has drawn. At a predetermined time later in the day, the child writes the word and its definition on the board for his classmates. After briefly discussing the word, have each student copy the word and its definition on the appropriate page in his word booklet. Continue the activity throughout the year, asking students to restock The Discovery Box as needed. By the end of the school year, students will have impressive word collections.

Leigh Anne Newsom—Gr. 3, Greenbrier Intermediate, Chesapeake, VA

22

Vocabulary Hunt

Write a word in each box.

an action word	a synonym for *old*	a descriptive word	a noun that has five or more letters	
a weather word	a synonym for *big*	a two-syllable word	a feeling	a synonym for *said*
a one-syllable word	a noun that has fewer than five letters	a word used in cooking	a compound word	a homograph
a contraction			a holiday word	a three-syllable word

All-Star Word Bird

Write a new vocabulary word in the box.
In each star, write a word or a phrase that tells about the word.

Awards

Duplicate and present these awards to students as desired.

has earned this

OFFICIAL WORD WATCHER AWARD

for spotting a new word.

Signed

Date

is a

WORD CHAMPION!

CONGRATULATIONS!

To:

From:

Because:

knows that learning new words is cool!

DICTIONARY

Now You're Cookin'!

A quick stop at Chef Nym's Snack Shack will increase your students' appetites for antonym and synonym practice. Using only prizewinning recipes, Chef Nym has prepared top-of-the-line activities, reproducibles, and ready-to-use activity cards to tantalize even the most wary taste buds!

ideas by Janice Bradley

A Tic-Tac-Toe Recipe

Tempt your students' taste buds with Chef Nym's new tic-tac-toe recipe. Draw and program the spaces of a tic-tac-toe grid with words having synonyms (or antonyms). Divide students into two teams. In turn, a player from each team chooses a word from the grid, then says that word and a synonym for it. If correct, the player draws his team's symbol *(X or O)* atop the word. The first team to have three symbols aligned horizontally, diagonally, or vertically on the grid scores one point. If the game is a draw, no point is scored. Draw and program a new grid to play each succeeding game. Continue play until one team reaches a predetermined score or game time is over.

Pizza By The Slice

Students will find it hard to resist slices of Chef Nym's mouthwatering pizza. In advance, have students color, cut out, and fold duplicated copies of the pizza pattern on page 27. Then gather and program each cutout with one word of an antonym (or synonym) pair. Seat students in a circle, redistribute the cutouts, and have each student secretly make note of his "pizza word." In turn, have individual students pantomime their words inside the circle. When a youngster believes the word being pantomimed is his word's antonym, he stands and declares, "Pizza delivery!" He must then identify the pantomimed word. If correct, the student shares his corresponding antonym and the two youngsters take side-by-side places in the circle. If the pantomimed word is misidentified, or if an incorrect match is made, the pantomiming student continues and the other youngster sits down. Continue in this manner until all matches have been made.

Order Up!

Cook up this card game in a matter of minutes. Label several construction-paper cards with words having antonyms (or synonyms). Also label each of several distractor cards with the words "Order Up" and decorate as desired. Combine and place cards facedown. In turn, each of two to four players draws a card, reads the word, and provides its antonym. If the answer is accepted by the remaining players, he keeps the card. He may then draw another card (and follow the same procedure) or pass the play to the next player. If his answer is not accepted, he returns the card to the bottom of the card pile. If an "Order Up!" card is drawn, a player must return all his cards to the bottom of the card pile. The winner is the student holding the most cards when game time is over.

Lona Ritchie, Perry County District #32, Perryville, MO

Snacks To Go

Chef Nym has even prepared a snack-to-go for each of your students! Duplicate student copies of the patterns on page 26 onto white construction paper. To make the hot dog (an antonym word bank), color, cut out, and fold the pattern. If desired, decorate the hot dog shape with condiments cut from construction-paper scraps. Then unfold and program the inside of the cutout with antonym pairs.

To make an order of fries (a synonym word bank), color, cut out, fold, and glue the fry envelope. Then cut out and trace the french fry pattern several times onto light tan construction paper. Cut out the resulting french fry shapes before programming each with a synonym pair. Store completed cutouts in the fry envelope.

For added fun, have students design Snack Shack carry-out bags by labeling and decorating light-colored lunch sacks. Advise each student to place his completed snack-to-go inside his bag for the trip home.

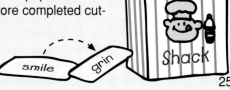

25

Patterns Use patterns with “Snacks To Go” on page 25.

Fold.

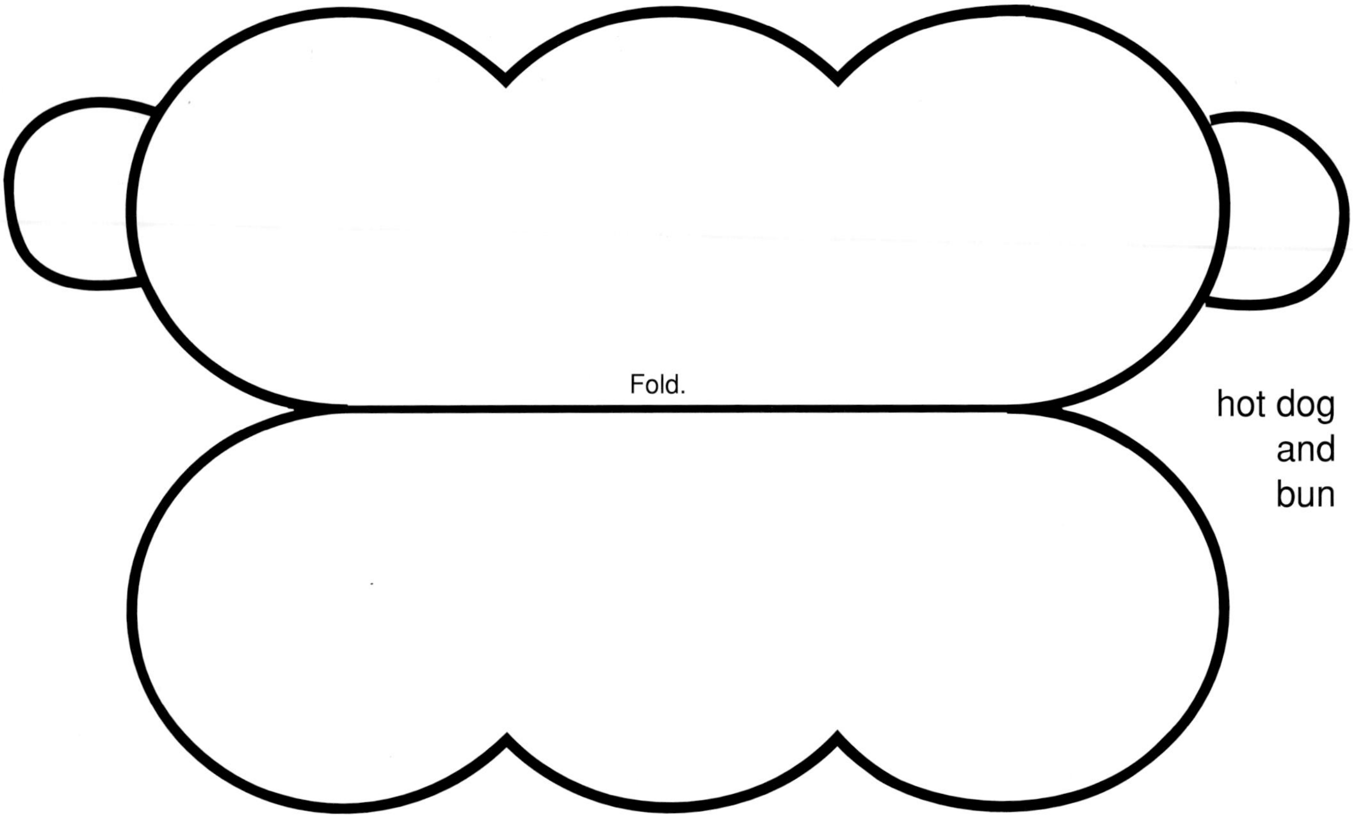

hot dog
and
bun

french fry

Glue.
Fold.
Glue.

french fry
envelope

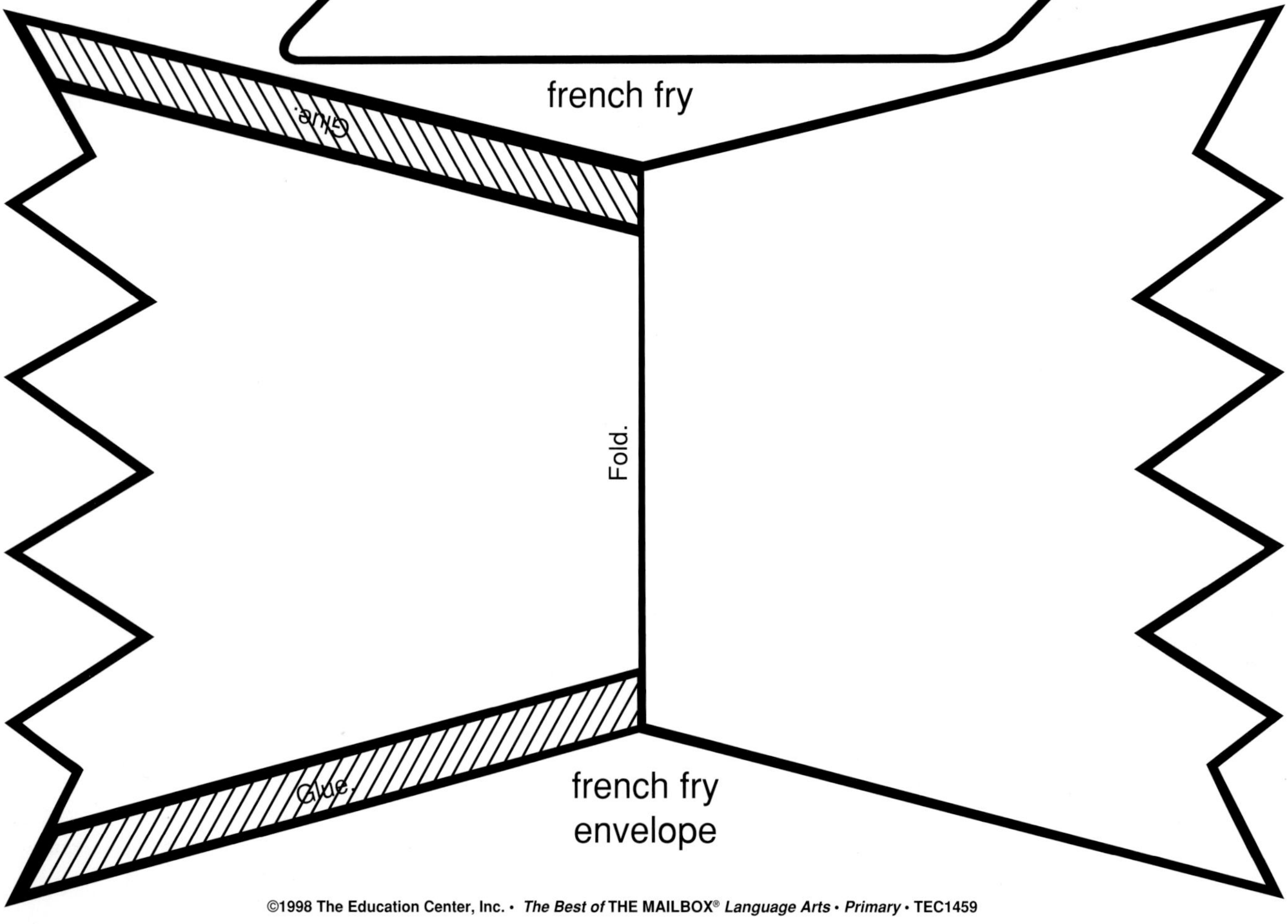

Fold.

Use with "Pizza By The Slice" on page 25.

Present copies of this award to students who have shown improvements in their synonym and/or antonym skills. **Award**

_____
Student

***has discovered
the recipe for***

_____ ***success!***
Antonym/Synonym

_____
Teacher

_____
Date

Name _____

Antonyms À La Mode

Write the antonyms.
Use the word bank.

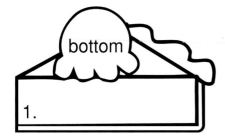
bottom
1.

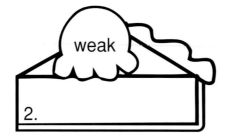
weak
2.

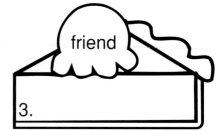
friend
3.

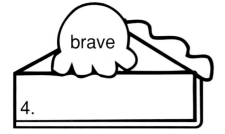
brave
4.

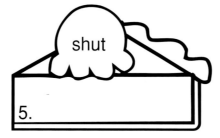
shut
5.

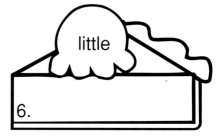
little
6.

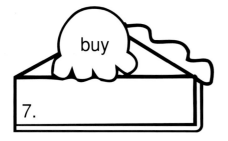
buy
7.

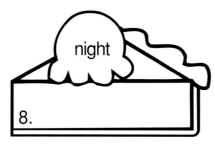
night
8.

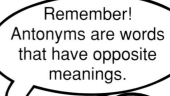
Remember! Antonyms are words that have opposite meanings.

awake
9.

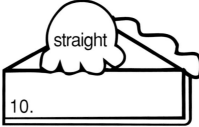
straight
10.

Chef Nym

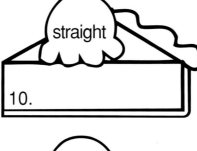
front
11.

play
12.

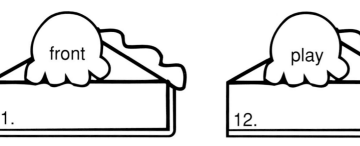
Bonus Box: *À la mode* means to be topped with ice cream. On the back of this sheet list five or more other foods that you think would be delicious if served à la mode.

Word Bank

asleep	big
enemy	back
curly	day
strong	sell
afraid	top
work	open

Name _____   Synonyms

Snacking On Synonyms

Cut.
Match and paste.

Remember! Synonyms are words that have about the same meanings.

Chef Nym

relax

hard

delicious   tasty

cost

happy

present

tidy

friend

quick

slash

start

©1998 The Education Center, Inc. • *The Best of* THE MAILBOX® *Language Arts* • *Primary* • TEC1459 • Key p. 159

price

Bonus Box: Draw and color a picture of your favorite snack food on the back of this sheet.

cut

fast

neat

rest

buddy

jolly

difficult

begin

gift

29

Synonyms and antonyms

Snack Shack Menu

Chef Nym

Snack Shack

Write the antonym.
Use the antonym word bank.

1.	candy	$1.50
	(sweet)	
2.	burger	$2.00
	(small)	
3.	sandwich	$2.50
	(hot)	
4.	hot dog	$1.75
	(short)	
5.	pizza	$2.50
	(thin)	
6.	ice cream	$.75
	(soft)	

Write the synonym.
Use the synonym word bank.

7.	sundae	$1.25
	(tiny)	
8.	pie	$1.25
	(tasty)	
9.	cone	$.75
	(enormous)	
10.	pretzels	$.75
	(skinny)	
11.	fries	$1.00
	(quick)	
12.	shake	$1.75
	(smooth)	

Antonym Word Bank

large	thick
long	sour
cold	hard

Synonym Word Bank

large	small
thin	delicious
fast	
creamy	

Bonus Box: Cut on the dotted lines. Fold the menu in half. Design and color the menu cover. Label it "Snack Shack."

Reading Motivation

Getting The Word Out

Creative Responses To Literature

Contrary to popular belief, you don't need magical powers or fancy gimmicks to get students interested in reading. Using these classroom-tested ideas, you'll discover that the best promoters you can find are right in your classroom. That's right! When students share their enthusiasm and opinions about books, other students listen. Start your reading campaign today and get the word out about reading!

Boasting About Books

When you discover a good book, most often you tell friends and co-workers about it. So why not give youngsters an opportunity to do something similar? Display a laminated poster to which you have attached a wipe-off marker. (See the illustration.) If a youngster wishes to tell his classmates about a book he's just read, he signs the poster. Set aside time each day for at least one student from the list to boast about his book. In addition to spreading the word about good books, your young boasters' self-esteems will be given a boost.

Diane Fortunato—Gr. 2
Carteret School
Bloomfield, NJ

I'm Ready To Boast About A Book!
Eileen
Sam
Ben
Cara
Selina

Book Of The Week

This year-round bulletin board is sure to turn some heads and some pages! Every week arrange for a different student to spotlight her favorite book at the display. Ask the student to design colorful banners and posters about her book, and to bring to school any appropriate objects mentioned in the book that could entice her classmates' reading interest. For example a box of cereal that contains a prize, a lunchbox, a white sneaker, and a sheet of blank drawing paper could attract reading interest in *Alexander And The Terrible, Horrible, No Good, Very Bad Day* by Judith Viorst (Aladdin Paperbacks, 1987). Make plans to spotlight one of your favorite childhood books, too!

Lyn Moiseff—Chapter I
Sullivan School
North Adams, MA

Pictures To Read By

Since young readers also like to color, these student-made coloring books are an ideal way to pique reading interest. First ask each student to tell her classmates about one of her favorite books. As each child takes her turn, write the student's name and the title of the book she is presenting on a half-sheet of paper. When all students have taken their turns, hand out the papers and have the youngsters draw pencil illustrations about the books they presented. Photocopy their illustrations—two per page—using the front and back of each page if desired. Collate the duplicated pages and staple them into individual coloring books. As students color in these keepsake coloring books, they are reminded of several good books to read!

Kay Wulf—Gr. 1, Cheney Elementary School, Cheney, KS

Top Ten Titles

Here's a trendy way to promote reading! At the end of each month, have students nominate books for a top ten list. Nominations can include books the students have read independently and books that have been read aloud to them during that month. Write the nominated titles on the board, limiting the number if necessary. Then, by class vote, determine your youngsters' top ten favorites. Copy the resulting list on a sheet of chart paper titled "Our Top Ten Books For The Month Of _____." Post the list in the hallway outside your classroom door. Also send a duplicated copy of the list home with each student.

Pamela Doerr—Substitute Teacher
Elizabethtown School District
Elizabethtown, PA

Our Top Ten Books
For The Month Of May
1. Charlotte's Web
2. Cloudy With A Chance Of Meatballs
3. Freckle Juice
4. Amelia Bedelia
5. Miss Nelson Is Back
6. Beezus And Ramona
7. The Beast In Miss Rooney's Room
8. Nate The Great
9. Doctor DeSoto
10. The Chocolate Touch

We'll Read To You!

Looking for reading motivation? This weekly reading extravaganza is sure to send your young readers into orbit! Set aside the same time each week for a variety of guests to visit your classroom for the purpose of being read to by your youngsters. The guests can include your youngsters' family members, retired teachers, school board members, community and school volunteers, residents of a senior-citizen community, and students from other classrooms in your school. Each week plan to have every youngster read aloud to at least one visitor. Ask the visitors to talk with the young readers to elicit the students' opinions and understanding of the books they are reading. These positive reading experiences build self-esteem and foster a joy of reading!

Phil Forsythe—Gr. 3
Northeastern Elementary School
Bellefontaine, OH

Book Editor Of The Week

Draw attention to new books, forgotten books, and favored books with this book-sharing idea. Each week choose one student to be the book editor of the week. This student shows his classmates five of his favorite books and reveals why he likes these books so much. Then he displays these books in a classroom area reserved for the weekly book editor's five favorite books. Invite students to peruse the books during their free time over the next five days. In just a few minutes each week, you can spark volumes of reading enthusiasm!

Pamela Doerr—Substitute Teacher

Swapping Books

At some time, most students have purchased or received paperback books. Once these books have been read, they're often stored on shelves and forgotten. To keep these books from gathering dust, plan periodic book swaps. Notify parents in advance and request that they help their children choose books they no longer wish to keep. Give each child one book buck (patterns on page 36) for each undamaged, grade-level-appropriate paperback book that he brings to school. Display the assortment of books, adding a few paperbacks from your class library if desired. Place the names of all participating students in a box; then determine the order in which students visit the book swap by drawing names from the box. The next time you plan a book swap, consider inviting another classroom or two to join in on the fun.

Barbara McIntyre—Gr. 2
Sacred Heart School
Lombard, IL

Name That Title!

Here's a fun twist to the traditional book report. Rather than initially revealing the title of the book she is reporting on, a student discloses interesting information about the book in the hopes that her classmates can name the book's title. For example, if a student is reporting on *Madeline* by Ludwig Bemelmans (Viking Penguin, 1996), she might begin by revealing that the story takes place in another country and that the main character is a young girl who attends a boarding school. If the book's title is quickly identified, the presenter shares a few more interesting facts about the story before she concludes her presentation. If the book's title is not identified, the student reveals it at the conclusion of her report. Now, that's a fun twist to an old standby!

Diane Fortunato—Gr. 2, Carteret School, Bloomfield, NJ

Seal Of Approval

For a student, the perfect book recommendation is to know that one of his classmates has given the book his seal of reading approval. Duplicate a supply of the reading seal on page 36. When a student wishes to give a book from the classroom library his seal of reading approval, he fills out a reading seal, cuts it out, and uses a paper clip to attach it to the book. Then he displays the book in an area reserved for student-approved books. Each student may attach his seal of reading approval to two books. When a student decides to approve a third book, he must remove his seal from one of his previously approved books. This fresh approach brings new life to your classroom library!

Susan Hamm—Gr. 3
Sacred Heart School
Florissant, MO

The Chocolate Touch

Keepsake Memory Boxes

Turn reading experiences into lasting memories with these special boxes. Each student needs a shoebox and lid or something similar. Ask an adult volunteer to help each child separately cover his box and lid with brightly colored paper. Then have the students personalize their containers as desired. Each time a child reads a book, he places in his box a nonperishable item that he feels represents or symbolizes the book in some way. For example a student who read *The Rainbow Fish* by Marcus Pfister (North-South Books, 1992) might place a small scale shape cut from foil or holographic gift wrap in his box. Periodically divide students into small groups. Ask each student to talk about one or two books he has recently read and show the members of his group the related keepsake(s) from his memory box. It's amazing how well students can recall the stories that they've read when they have concrete objects to jog their memories. These memories are sure to pique additional reading interest among the students' peers, too!

Clare Czachowski
Deer Park, TX

On Cue

Oral book reflections are perfect for enhancing speaking and comprehension skills. In addition, they are also a fun way for students to keep abreast of what their classmates are reading. Prepare several cue cards like the one shown for students to use during their presentations. You may wish to design different versions of the card. For example some cards can be specifically for fiction titles, while others can be for nonfiction titles or books of poetry. Keep the cards where they are easily accessible to students. Every so often take a "commercial break" during a period of transition, and ask a student volunteer to reflect upon a book he's recently read. To do this, the volunteer chooses an appropriate cue card and follows the cues!

Barbara B. MacArthur—Gr. 3, St. Mary Magdalen School
Wilmington, DE

Meet The Molesons

One of my favorite illustrations shows the kids and their mother in bed with fake chicken pox!

Book Talk Cue Card
1. Title
2. Author
3. Description of main character
4. Description of setting
5. Share favorite words and/or favorite illustrations
6. "I would/would not recommend this book because..."

Thumbs-Up, Thumbs-Down

Students get a kick out of this weekly book-review event—and so might Siskel and Ebert! Each week ask a different pair of students to choose a book they'd both like to read and review. Each of the students reads and reviews the book independently; then, the following week, the two reviewers face their classmates and share their opinions about the book they both read. Encourage reviewers to comment on specific book elements such as the characterization, plot, and setting; give their opinions about the overall appeal of the book; and tell if the book met their expectations. Encourage the two reviewers to interact with each other, but at the same time, caution them to be accepting of the other reviewer's opinions. Then have each reviewer give the book a thumbs-up or a thumbs-down rating. Whatever the outcome, these books will be hot items in the library for weeks to come.

Dianne Neumann—Gr. 2
Frank C. Whiteley School
Hoffman Estates, IL

Reading Recommendations

Motivate students to make reading recommendations for their classmates with a collection of inexpensive photo albums and a supply of duplicated forms like the one shown. Label the albums with book categories such as "Marvelous Mysteries," "All About Animals," "Rib-Tickling Tales," and "Fact-Filled Books." Then ask each student to complete a reading recommendation as a homework assignment. Review the forms and have students make any necessary changes. Then have the students place their completed recommendations in the appropriate photo albums.

Encourage students to write recommendations when they read books that they think their classmates would enjoy. Caution students to always check the appropriate albums first to verify that the books they are considering have not been previously recommended. These student-published albums are wonderful resources, and they are fun for students to read, too!

Dianne Neumann—Gr. 2

I'd Like To Share This
Book With You!
Recommendation by: _____
Title Of My Book: _____
Author: _____
This book is _____

This picture shows _____

Books On Parade

One surefire way to spread a reading epidemic is to stage a "Books On Parade." Ask each child to think about a book he recently read and enjoyed. Then, in a note sent home, inform parents which day you'd like the youngsters to come to school dressed as book characters from their chosen books. Ask that each student carry a sign labeled with the title and author of the book he is representing. Also encourage parents and students to keep costumes simple. On the day of the event, plan time for each student to introduce his chosen book personality to his classmates and say a few words about the corresponding book. Then arrange for students to parade through other selected classrooms and, if possible, repeat their book-related spiels. For additional reading motivation, join forces with your teaching colleagues and plan a grade-level or schoolwide promenade.

Linda Zook—Gr. 2
Our Lady Of The Assumption School
Lethbridge, Alberta
Canada

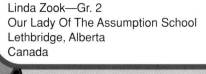

Amelia Bedelia

Dr. DeSoto

Freckle Juice

Patterns Use book bucks with "Swapping Books" on page 33.

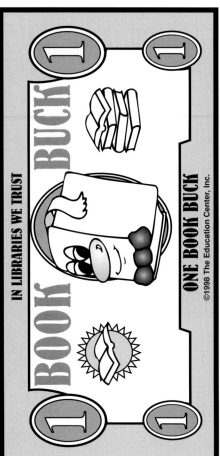

Use with "Seal Of Approval" on page 34.

A HARVEST OF READING MOTIVATION

You've planted the seed of reading knowledge and you're busy cultivating your students' reading skills. What more could you use? How about a bumper crop of reading motivation? Implement your favorite ideas from this collection, and in no time your budding readers will be blooming with reading enthusiasm!

Books And Backpacks

Boost reading enthusiasm and self-esteem with books and backpacks! Each week distribute a backpack to two or three different students. Help each youngster select and place in his backpack a book from the school or classroom library that he would like to read aloud to others. Also place a copy of a parent note in each backpack that explains the following procedure: On Monday and Tuesday evenings, the student practices reading his selected book aloud to his family members. Also encourage each student to gather (or create) story props and to use the props to enhance his presentation of the book. On Wednesday the backpack (containing the book and story props) is returned to school and the student rehearses his book presentation with you. On Thursday the student presents his book to another staff member, and on Friday he chooses to give his book presentation to either his classmates or to another class of his own choice. You can count on reading enthusiasm to soar right along with your students' self-confidence!

Michelle Dunnam—Gr. 2
Haskell Elementary School
Haskell, TX

Literary Door Displays

Get the word out about reading with this schoolwide plan! To begin, ask each class to decorate the outside of its hallway door to spotlight a favorite book. Require that each door decoration include the title of the chosen book. Then, on a predetermined day, ask all teachers to close their hallway doors so that each class of students can take a turn viewing the door displays throughout the school. Students are sure to discover several books that they'd like to read or have read to them! Repeat this schoolwide door-decorating activity as often as you like. To encourage a variety of reading, designate book categories or themes like animal stories, tall tales, fairy tales, nonfiction books, and biographies for future decorating projects.

Andrea Isom Burzlaff—Gr. 3, Coventry School, Crystal Lake, IL
Hope H. Taylor—Gr. 3, Birchcrest School, Bellevue, NE

Mystery Readers

Mystery readers are a foolproof plan for spreading reading enthusiasm! Throughout the year make arrangements for your students' parents and a variety of other community members to read aloud to your class. If desired, provide each reader with a list of suggested literature and request that each guest confirm in advance his or her reading selection to avoid repetitions. On the day that a mystery reader is scheduled to visit, write the words "Mystery Reader" on the chalkboard. Students will eagerly anticipate the mystery reader's visit. With this plan, students are exposed to a variety of books and reading styles, and they quickly discover that books are enjoyed by many people!

Krista K. Zimmerman—Gr. 3
Tuckerton Elementary School
Tuckerton, NJ

Bookish Vests

Your youngsters will be dressed for reading success when they wear these student-decorated vests. For each student sew a simple fabric vest or cut a vest from a large paper grocery bag. Personalize the inside of each child's vest; then store the vests for safekeeping. You will also need a supply of patches cut from iron-on Pellon® (for fabric vests) or construction paper (for paper vests). Each time you wrap up a series of activities that relate to a specific book, have each student decorate a patch that highlights the book. To do this a student uses colorful markers to label his patch with the book's title and author, and then he illustrates his favorite scene from the book. If students are decorating fabric vests, collect the completed patches and iron them onto the vests at a later time. Students can glue the paper patches in place themselves. Your students will love wearing these vests and sharing the attached book recommendations with others.

Sandy Greensfelder—Gr. 1
Naples Elementary
Naples, Italy

Reading Through Your State

Promote a love of literature with a state reading campaign! Create a simple outline of your state that shows each county; then duplicate and distribute a class supply of the resulting map. Or enlarge and post one map for the entire class. The goal of this reading project is for students to read their way through their home state. To do this, allow students to color in one county for every 30 minutes (or other designated time increment) of independent reading. The project is complete when the state map is entirely colored. If desired, plan to share interesting facts about each of your state's counties during the campaign. Once your state reading campaign is finished, challenge students to read their way through the United States—state by state. Wow! Reading really *does* take you places!

Karen Hertges—Gr. 3
C. F. S. Catholic Elementary School
Spillville, IA

Reading Can't Be Beat!

March your students into independent reading with this motivational display. Mount the title "Reading Can't Be Beat!" and several colorful music-note cutouts on a bulletin board. Also duplicate a white construction-paper copy of the bookmark pattern on page 40 for each child. Have each student personalize a bookmark, cut out the shape, punch a hole in the top of the cutout where indicated, and tie a loop of yarn through the hole. Use pushpins to display the bookmarks as shown. When a child finishes reading a book, he writes the title and author of the book on his posted bookmark. When all the spaces on his bookmark are filled, he prepares another bookmark and uses a second loop of yarn to connect his two cutouts. Students will enjoy checking out each other's lists for book suggestions, and you'll have a complete record of each student's independent reading efforts. Now, isn't that music to your ears?

Linda Madron—Gr. 1
Mary D. Lang Elementary
Kennett Square, PA

CHECK OUT THESE BO...
The Missing Fossil Mystery
Author: Emily Herman
Title: The Skates Of Uncle Richard
Author: Carol Fenner
Title:
Author:
Title:
Author:
Title:
Author:
Title:
Author:
Name Zack Pilley

The Reading Train

Keep your students' interest in reading right on track with this colorful classroom display! Mount an engine cutout and the title "Choo-Choo-Choose A Book To Read!" on a classroom wall. Duplicate a construction-paper supply of the train-car pattern on page 41. Then set aside one or more times per week for students to tell their classmates about the books they've recently read. Each time a student tells the class about a different book, give him a train-car pattern to complete and cut out. Mount the students' completed cutouts end-to-end behind the engine. As your students' interest in reading grows, so will your class train! At the end of the year, dismantle the class train and staple each student's train cars together to create a shape booklet of the books he read during the school year. All aboard for reading!

Robyn Dill—Gr. 1
Northwestern Elementary
Kokomo, IN

Reading Reactions

Reader-reaction cards are sure to pique additional reading interest among your students! Secure a Press-On Pocket to the inside back cover of each book in your classroom library; then slip a lined index card inside each pocket. After reading a book, a student writes his comments about the book on the provided reader-reaction card, then signs and dates the card. To get the project rolling, write a variety of book-related comments on several of the cards. Students will be eager to read your remarks, read the books you've read, and add their own reactions to the cards. Now, that's a surefire way to start a reading epidemic!

Jana Atchley—Education Student
Johnson Bible College
Knoxville, TN

A Family Affair

This year-round reading plan nurtures reading relationships between students and their parents. You'll need to invest some time and energy in the initial preparations, but once the plan is in place it requires minimal effort to manage.

To prepare your book collection, number each book, and then number a large resealable plastic bag to match. Place each book inside its bag. To make an instruction/comment booklet for each of the resulting book bags, fold a 9" x 12" sheet of construction paper in half. Glue a signed copy of the parent letter (page 42) to the front cover; then unfold the construction paper and glue a copy of the project guidelines (also on page 42) to the left-hand side. If desired, laminate the project for durability; then use a brad fastener to secure several pages of blank or lined paper to the right-hand side of the opened booklet. Close the booklet. Number one booklet for each book bag; then seal the booklets inside the book bags.

To create a record-keeping system, duplicate a supply of the reading record on page 41. You will also need student copies of a number list that corresponds to your book collection. To make a check-out folder for each student, attach a copy of the reading record and the number list to a sheet of construction paper, and then fold the construction paper in half as shown. Ask each child to personalize her folder and store it for safekeeping in a designated location.

To check out a book bag, a student writes the bag number and current date in his check-out folder. When he returns the book bag, he records the date of return and circles the corresponding number in his folder. Assist students with this record-keeping procedure until they grow accustomed to it. When a student has filled each space on his reading record, staple a second reading record atop the completed one. Students will enjoy taking books home to share with their parents; parents will enjoy seeing their students' reading skills improve; and you will feel confident that your students are soaring toward reading success!

Linh Tran—Gr. 1
Wallace Elementary, York, PA

CHECK OUT THESE BOOKS!

Title: _____

Author: _____

Title: _____

Author: _____

Title: _____

Author: _____

Title: _____

Author: _____

Title: _____

Author: _____

Title: _____

Author: _____

Name _____

©1998 The Education Center, Inc. • *The Best of* THE MAILBOX® *Language Arts* • *Primary* • TEC1459

THE READING TRAIN

Name _____

Book Title: _____

Author: _____

Date: _____

©1998 The Education Center, Inc. • *The Best of* THE MAILBOX® *Language Arts* • *Primary* • TEC1459

Use the reading record with "A Family Affair" on page 39.

Name _____

MY READING RECORD

Book Number	Date Checked Out	Date Checked In	Book Number	Date Checked Out	Date Checked In

©1998 The Education Center, Inc. • *The Best of* THE MAILBOX® *Language Arts* • *Primary* • TEC1459

Parent Letter And Project Guidelines

Use with "A Family Affair" on page 39.

IT'S A FAMILY AFFAIR!

Project Guidelines

1. Please handle every book with care.

2. If a book is damaged, tell your teacher when you return the book.

3. After you have read the book, write your name, the date, and a comment about the book on the paper to the right.

4. Return this bag of materials to the classroom when you are finished reading the book and writing your comment. You may then select another book bag to take home!

Dear Parent,

Your child is participating in our classroom Family Affair Reading Project. The goal of this project is for each child to spend quality time reading together with a family member.

Please take time to enjoy this book with your child. Remember that the books in our classroom library vary in difficulty. Your child will find some books more challenging than others. Do not worry if your child needs help reading a book. It is perfectly fine for you to provide reading assistance. Or you may choose to read the book aloud to your child.

Inside this folder you will find a few simple guidelines for your child to follow. I hope you and your child have a wonderful time reading together!

Sincerely,

Giant Bookmarks

idea by Debbie M. Lee, Clarendon Hills, IL

Although making these larger-than-life bookmarks is a great creative outlet for your students, the benefits of making and using them go far beyond the cosmetic appeal. Once students begin to indicate their favorite books on their bookmarks, youngsters can also see for themselves which types of books they most enjoy and which types of books they have neglected to try recently. If the bookmarks are prominently displayed, youngsters with similar interests are likely to notice the titles that are their classmates' favorites and take the hint from them about some books to consider for future reading.

To start this program, give each student a 6" x 18" (or larger) strip of tagboard. Have him decorate a 1 3/4-inch border all around the bookmark with designs that represent his interests. Encourage creativity by supplying students with materials to make crayon-resist, glue-resist, collage, mosaic, stamped, or stenciled designs, for example. Once the bookmarks have been designed and personalized, attach from the top of each bookmark a length of ribbon, yarn, or other material. Display these bookmarks where the artwork can be admired, the titles can be read, and students can easily add titles.

Once a student has read a book that he could highly recommend to his friends, have him cut out and complete the appropriate slip (page 44). Have him glue the slip within the decorative borders of his bookmark. Once most of the available space within the borders has been occupied by slips, encourage students to align additional slips atop the ones already in place. Caution students to glue these additional slips along only the left side so that the slips may be flipped up for viewing those beneath.

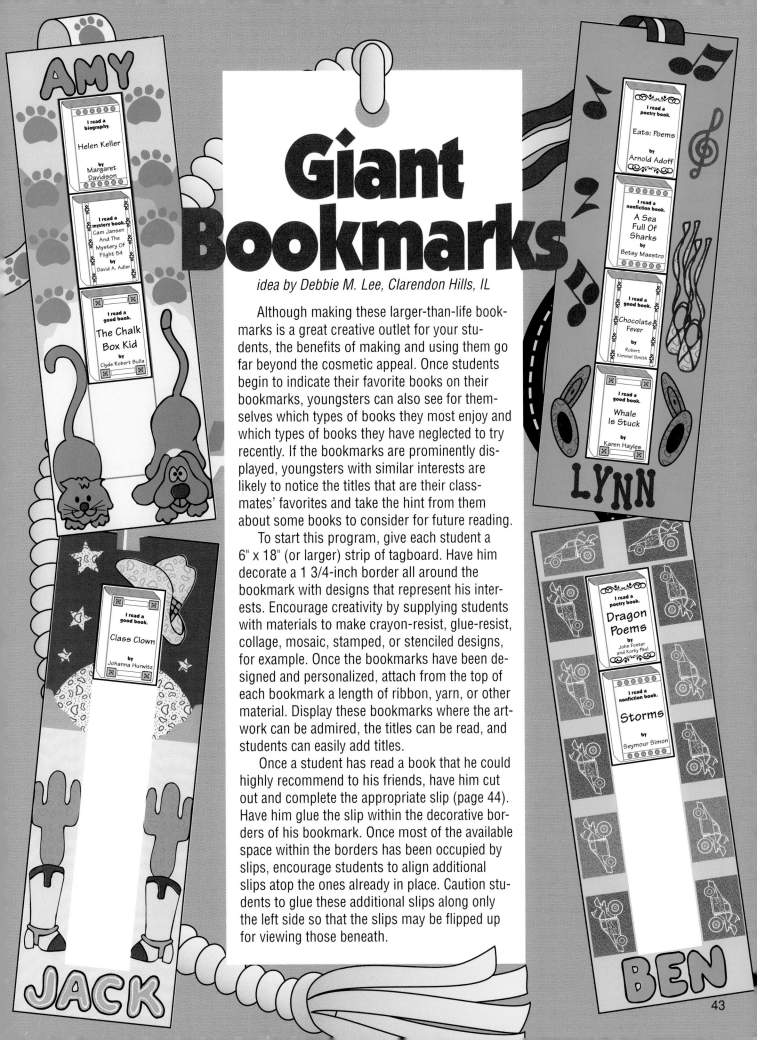

AMY

I read a biography.
Helen Keller
by Margaret Davidson

I read a mystery book.
Cam Jansen And The Mystery Of Flight 54
by David A. Adler

I read a good book.
The Chalk Box Kid
by Clyde Robert Bulla

I read a good book.
Class Clown
by Johanna Hurwitz

JACK

LYNN

I read a poetry book.
Eats: Poems
by Arnold Adoff

I read a nonfiction book.
A Sea Full Of Sharks
by Betsy Maestro

I read a good book.
Chocolate Fever
by Robert Kimmel Smith

I read a good book.
Whale Is Stuck
by Karen Hayles

BEN

I read a poetry book.
Dragon Poems
by John Foster and Korky Paul

I read a nonfiction book.
Storms
by Seymour Simon

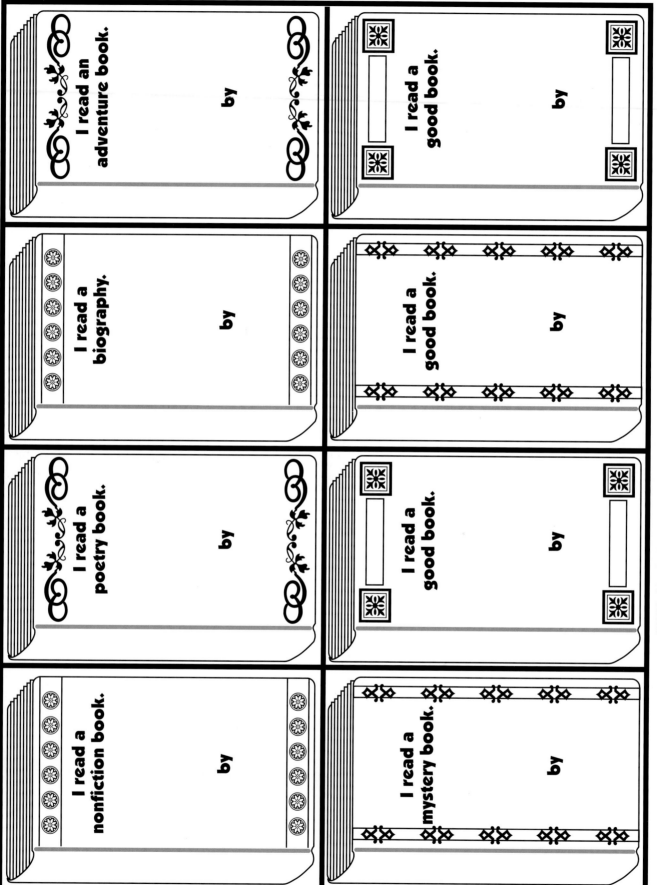

I read an adventure book.

by

I read a good book.

by

I read a biography.

by

I read a good book.

by

I read a poetry book.

by

I read a good book.

by

I read a nonfiction book.

by

I read a mystery book.

by

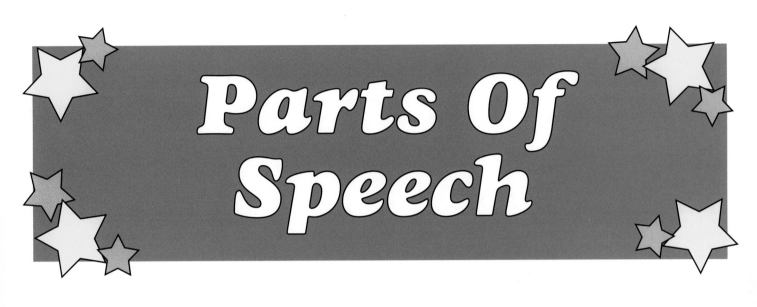

Parts Of Speech

OPERATION N.O.U.N.

Appoint your students "secret agents"; then enlist their help with this special undercover assignment. Operation N.O.U.N. entails identifying, naming, classifying, and using common and proper nouns. The following activities, reproducibles, ready-to-use file folder, pattern, and award are certain to help your agents crack this case!

ideas by Mary Anne Haffner and Sue Ireland

Secret Agent Serenade

Add to the fun of this undercover assignment by teaching your secret agents the Operation N.O.U.N. theme song. It's sure to build enthusiasm and provide an inside track on noun identification! Have agents serenade to the tune of "Old MacDonald Had A Farm."

I spy nouns, oh yes I do.
N-O-U-N-S.
Names of people, places, and things—
N-O-U-N-S.
With a common noun here,
And a proper noun there.
Here's a name, there's a name.
Everywhere are more names.
I spy nouns, oh yes I do.
N-O-U-N-S.

A Spy Ring

Secret agents put their noun know-how to the test with this fast-paced category game. Have agents form a large ring in an open area of the classroom. Call out a noun category such as person (place or thing). In turn each agent calls out a noun from that category. If an agent repeats a previously used noun or gives an incorrect answer, he goes to the center of the ring. He leaves the center when another agent takes his place. For an added challenge, have agents name nouns from the following categories: plural, singular, common, proper.

"Eye" Spy

You won't find agents hiding behind newspapers during this undercover mission. Quite the contrary—agents will be spying *at* the newspaper! Provide newspaper sections for student pairs. Using crayons, each pair circles as many nouns as possible during a predetermined amount of time. When time is called, pair the twosomes and instruct each to read their noun selections to the other. One point is earned for each noun that is read correctly. As noun identification skills are strengthened, challenge agent pairs to locate specific noun types such as common, proper, singular, or plural.

Nouns In Disguise

Could nouns be lurking within the names of your secret agents? This mission will lead to the answer! Instruct each agent to write his full name at the top of his paper. Then, using only the letters in his name, have each agent find hidden nouns. Inform agents that letters may be used out of order and individual letters may be doubled. Each agent lists the nouns he finds on his paper. To extend the activity, have agents color-code their lists by instructing them to circle the kinds of nouns (person, place or thing) using crayons of different colors.

Top Secret Documents

New names, new disguises, and visiting new places are all part of going undercover. And, of course, this information must remain top secret! Provide each agent with three 6" x 9" sheets of differently colored construction paper. Agents label their "top secret documents" as follows: Undercover Names, Places Seen, Supplies Used. From newspapers and magazines, each agent cuts pictures and words to glue on the documents that reveal his undercover involvement.

Since top secret documents should never be left unattended, a briefcase may be in order! For complete instructions see "Baffled By The Briefcase!"

Baffled By The Briefcase!

Keep top secret documents out of sight with this easy-to-make briefcase. Fold a 12" x 18" sheet of brown construction paper twice as shown (Step 1). Glue the lower edges together to form a pocket. Fold, then cut away the center of a 4 1/2" x 6" piece of brown construction paper without cutting through the fold (Step 2). Glue the loose ends of the cutout to the top of the folded construction paper (Step 3). To make a latch, trim a construction-paper scrap to the desired size, and glue the lower half of the cutout to the front of the briefcase (Step 4).

Step 1
Step 2
Step 3
Step 4

Who Goes There?

Agents must conceal their identities to complete this undercover mission. In the center of a sheet of drawing paper, each agent draws and colors a self-portrait. Next, using construction-paper scraps, he creates and glues a disguise atop his portrait. The agent then writes nouns that begin with each letter of his name randomly around the paper. In addition, he writes five more words on his paper that are not nouns. Gather and redistribute the papers. Agents identify the disguised agents by crossing out the five words that are not nouns, then using the first letters of the remaining nouns to construct the names of the disguised.

Undercover Signals

Sharp minds and quick hands allow agents to quickly identify nouns to the CIA (chief of intelligent answers—you!). For each word called out, agents respond with thumbs-up (this word is a noun) or thumbs-down (this word is not a noun).

To vary the game, call out words that are nouns. Have agents respond using one of the following sets of hand signals:

one finger	= This noun is a singular.		tap shoulder	= This noun is the name of a person.
two fingers	= This noun is a plural.		point to ceiling	= This noun is the name of a place.
			knock on desk	= This noun is the name of a thing.

Secret Agent I.D.

Undercover identification keeps secret agents in hot pursuit of nouns. Duplicate student copies of the identification card on page 48. Each student writes his undercover name on the blank, draws his undercover identity in the small box, and mounts his card on a 6" x 9" sheet of black construction paper. He then folds his identification card in half and decorates the outside cover using construction-paper scraps. Students attach foil stars (earned by completing satisfactory noun assignments) to the empty box inside their I.D. cards. When a predetermined number of stars are earned, award students with special privileges, treats, or the award on page 48.

Use the I.D. card and award with "Secret Agent I.D." on page 47.

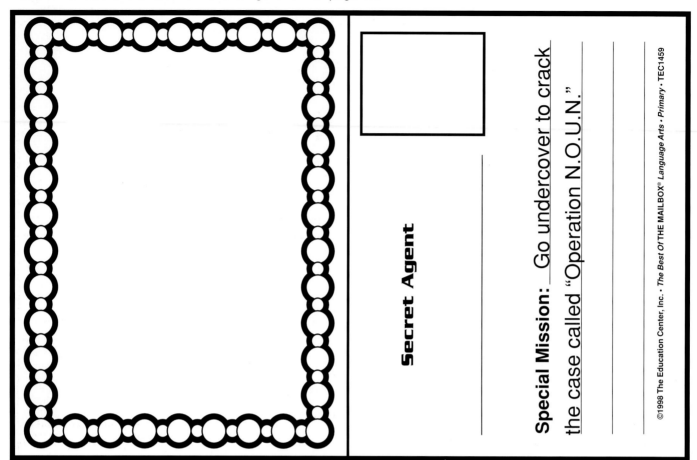

Secret Agent

Special Mission: Go undercover to crack the case called "Operation N.O.U.N."

©1998 The Education Center, Inc. • *The Best Of* THE MAILBOX® *Language Arts • Primary •* TEC1459

There's No Keeping This Under Our Hats!

Secret Agent

_____

is a master at noun identification!

We Knew You Could Do It!

CIA (Chief Of Intelligent Answers)   Date

©1998 The Education Center, Inc. • *The Best Of* THE MAILBOX® *Language Arts • Primary •* TEC1459

Name _____

The "Proper" Identification

Each word of a proper noun begins with a capital letter.
Write each proper noun correctly on a spy badge.
Use the code to color the stars on each badge.

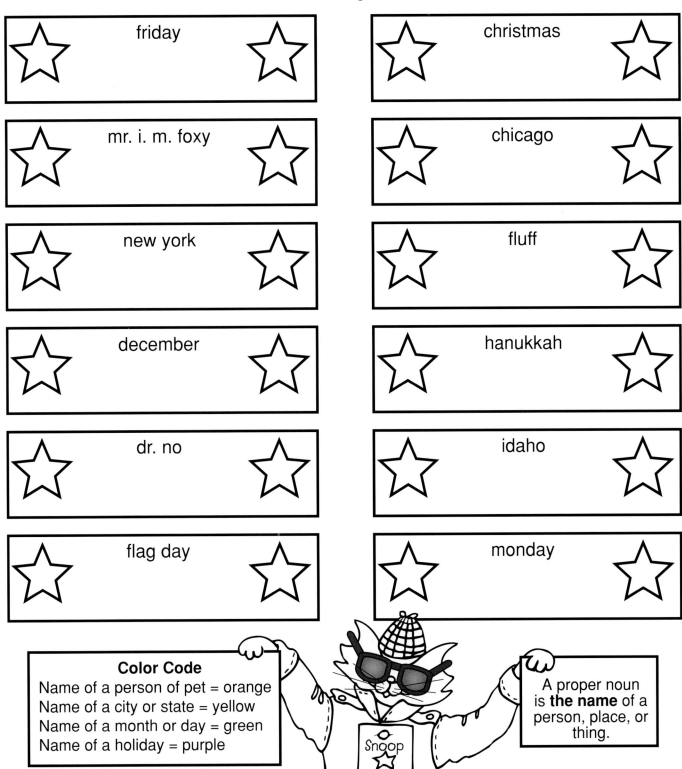

friday

christmas

mr. i. m. foxy

chicago

new york

fluff

december

hanukkah

dr. no

idaho

flag day

monday

Color Code
Name of a person of pet = orange
Name of a city or state = yellow
Name of a month or day = green
Name of a holiday = purple

Snoop

A proper noun is **the name** of a person, place, or thing.

Bonus Box: Make a spy badge like Snoop's! Cut a square from a piece of drawing paper. Write your name, and draw and color a star on the square. Cut a slit in the square and button it on your coat!

Name _____

Top Secret!

Spy Guy has several top secret assignments for you.
Each time you complete an assignment, color its folder.

10
Draw a spy cartoon. Underline each noun you use in the "talking part." Use three or more nouns.

15
Finish this story. When you are finished writing, underline the nouns you used.
"The name is Pond—James Pond," croaked the frog.

5
List five places a spy might visit.

10
Write ten nouns that you think a spy must know how to read.

5
List five things a spy might carry with him.

15
Write one proper noun that begins with each letter of the alphabet. Remember to use capital letters!

10
Cut ten nouns from a newspaper. Glue them onto a sheet of paper. Draw a blue box around each singular noun. Draw a red circle around each plural noun.

5
List five names that a spy might like to have.

20
Create an alphabet code. Use the code to write a secret message. Ask a friend to decode your message. Be sure to give him the secret code you created!

5
Write a spy joke or riddle. Use these nouns in your joke: elephant, sunglasses.

What kind of a spy are you?
Add the numbers in the colored folders.
Read the spy chart.

Spy Chart

80–100	=	A super sneak! Case is solved!
50–75	=	You've almost solved the case!
25–45	=	You're hot on the trail!
20 or less	=	Oops! Your cover is blown!

Bonus Box: Make a construction-paper folder for your work. Label the front of the folder "TOP SECRET!"

Staying In Tune With Verbs!

This collection of "action-packed" activities and reproducibles is brought to you by the one and only José Chameleono! A world-renowned chameleon, José specializes in reinforcing verb identification and usage skills. So hang onto your sombrero and join the fun! There's plenty of action for everyone!

ideas contributed by Mary Anne Haffner and Sue Ireland

A Piece Of The Action

José proclaims the best way to reinforce verbs as action words is to get a piece of the action! Make a duplicate set of easy-to-act-out verb cards. Have students form two lines facing each other. Distribute one set of cards to the students in each line. Instruct one line of students to act out their verb cards. Challenge each student in the second line to pair up with the student acting out the verb on his card. In turn, have each student pair act out its verb, then use its verb in a sentence. Have classmates identify the verb. Sort and redistribute the cards for another round of action.

Supplying The Action

Students must quickly brainstorm action words to play this fast-paced verb game. On each of several sheets of construction paper, mount a piece of a subject such as a monkey, teacher, airplane, baby, fireman, truck, or cowboy. Label each sheet with a corresponding sentence starter such as "The baby _____." Divide the students into five teams. One at a time, ask each team to come to the front of the room. Give the team a picture card and 15 seconds to study the card before beginning play. Facing their classmates, the team members (in turn) complete the sentence starter by supplying appropriate verbs. A team member may "pass" if he is unable to respond. Tally the number of sentences each team completes in one minute. The game is a great warm-up for verb lessons. Encourage students to submit pictures, and you'll soon have an assortment of playing cards.

The Changeable Chameleono

José's talents can aid students as they learn about different verb forms. Just as a chameleon changes colors to match his surroundings, verbs change forms to match their subjects or to indicate past, present, and future tenses. Give students a daily verb challenge by displaying a large cutout of José holding a verb card. To make the cutout, enlarge, color, and cut out the drawing of José on page 53. Have each student write sentences to show the past, present, and future tenses of the verb displayed, or to show the singular and plural verb forms. Younger students can orally provide sentences for specific forms. Change the verb card daily. Increase the challenge of the task by displaying a verb with an irregular verb form.

Read All About It!

Get parents involved in your verb study with this homework activity. Ask each student to work with a parent to compose a list of ten action verbs. Specify that the lists must include actions the parents were involved in during their day. On the following day, have students write and illustrate paragraphs titled "A Day In The Life Of [parent's name or title]," using their lists as verb banks. Challenge students to use each verb from their lists, but allow them to change the form or tense when necessary.

To extend the activity, have each student adjust his verb list so only the verbs used in his story are listed. Instruct each student to label his completed paragraph and verb list with a specific number. Display the paragraphs in numerical order, and compile the verb lists in numerical order to make an answer key. To reinforce verb identification, have students read the paragraphs and list the verbs used, then check their work using the answer key.

Win, Lose, Or Pantomime

This parts-of-speech game tickles José's funny bone! Label cards with simple sentences that contain action verbs such as "The cat jumped in the car." Divide students into two teams and write **noun** and **verb** on the chalkboard. Have a player from team one come to the front of the room. Show him a sentence card; then write the sentence on the board, substituting all nouns and verbs with blanks. The player attempts to pantomime the missing words. The player must indicate if he is pantomiming a noun or a verb by pointing to the chalkboard. Record each word when it is guessed. If the team correctly completes the sentence in three minutes, it earns five points. If not, team two has 30 seconds to confer and make a guess. A correct guess earns five points. Begin the next round with a player from team two. Continue alternating play between the teams. The team earning the most points wins.

Staying In Tune

Encourage students to use a wide variety of verbs with this eye-catching display. Brainstorm a long list of verbs. Have each student record specific verbs on large construction-paper note cutouts. Mount the cutouts along with an enlarged and colored cutout of José Chameleono (enlarge drawings on page 54). Title the display "Staying In Tune With Verbs." Encourage students to complete additional cutouts for display.

Where's The Action?

A word that shows action is called an **action verb.**

| Start | sell | pretty | cat | hide |

Find the action verbs.
An action verb will fit in this sentence:
José can _____ the guitar.

Color the squares.
Use the code below.

shake

every

| zoo | never | swing | | play |

| like | | lift | hold | strum | pink |

clean

Color Code
If the word shows **action**, color the square blue.
If the word **does not** show **action**, color the square green.

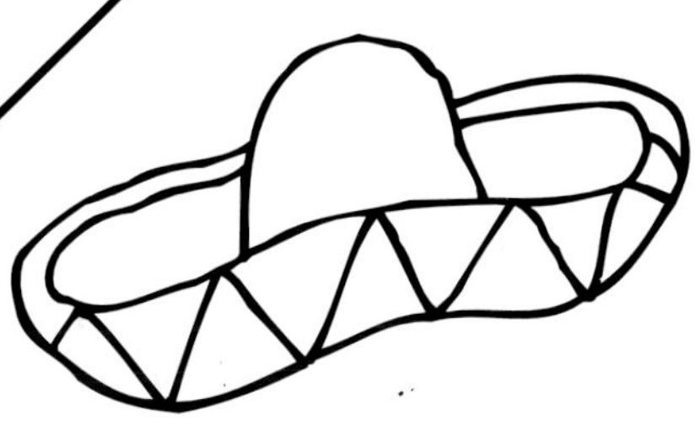

| people | buy | carry | both | Finish |

Bonus Box: Use this page as a gameboard! Label ten cards with action verbs and ten cards with words that are not action verbs. Ask a friend to play. Place your markers on start. Take turns drawing cards. If the word is a verb, move to a blue space. If the word is not a verb, move to a green space. The first player to reach finish wins!

In Tune With Verbs

Circle the verb in each sentence.
Write the verbs in the matching notes.
Use the code below to color the notes.

1. José looked for a book about chameleons.
2. The librarian helped José.
3. José finished the book in one day.
4. Now he knows a lot about chameleons!
5. Most chameleons live in Africa.
6. They climb trees.
7. Chameleons wrap their tails around tree branches.
8. A chameleon sees very well.
9. It watches its prey carefully.
10. One green chameleon climbed a big tree.
11. It watched a bug closely.
12. Then the chameleon pushed out its long sticky tongue.
13. The chameleon's tongue captured the bug!
14. Chameleons like bugs!
15. Chameleons change colors, too.
16. José liked the book about chameleons.

Color Code
past-tense verb = red
present-tense verb = yellow

©1998 The Education Center, Inc. • *The Best Of* THE MAILBOX® *LANGUAGE ARTS* • *Primary* • TEC1459 • Key p. 159

Name _____

Spin A Tune!

Help José complete his new song titles.
Cut around the circle shape.
Use a brad to fasten the shape to a paper plate.
Write a verb from the verb box in each slot as shown.
Read the new titles.
Spin the wheel and make more new titles!

Verb Box

Broke	Ate
Popped	Lost
Threw	Dropped
Found	Washed

Paper plate

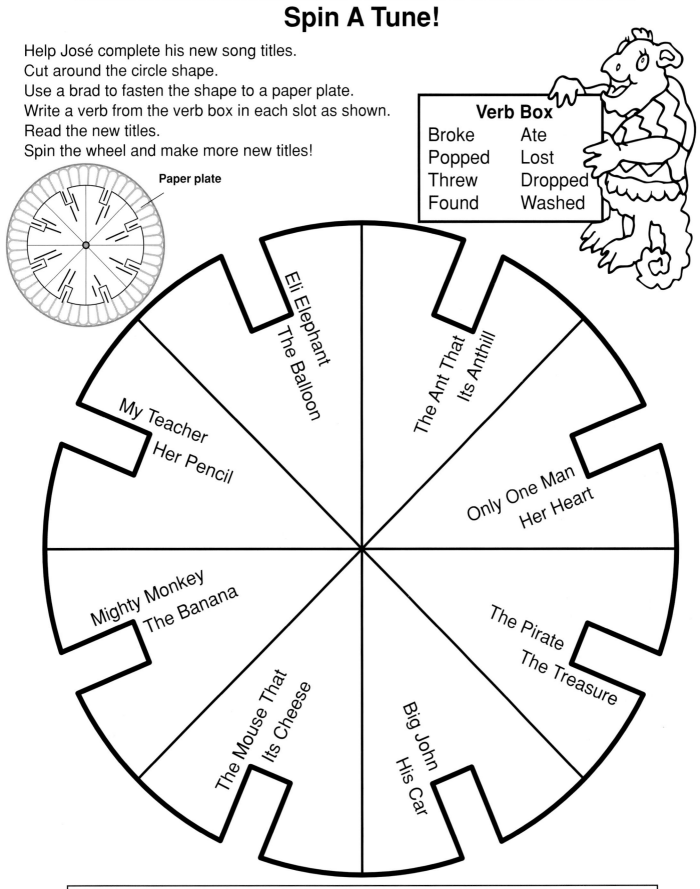

Bonus Box: Spin the wheel. Stop when all the slots are empty. Write a past-tense verb in each slot.
Read your new titles!

Note To Teacher: Each student will need a dinner-sized paper plate and a brad. Duplicate worksheet on heavy paper for best results.

Fine-

Introduce adjectives to your youngsters using the following activities and reproducibles. In no time at all, your youngsters will be strutting their descriptive writing skills and you'll feel proud as a peacock!

Peacock Word Banks

Fill these student-made word banks with descriptive adjectives! Using the patterns on page 60, duplicate student copies of the peacock body pattern onto white construction paper. Also duplicate a supply of feathers onto colorful construction paper. To make a word bank, trim, color, and mark a six-inch paper plate as shown. Cut out several feathers and punch a hole in each one at the dot. Stack the feathers; then insert a brad through the stack and through the **X** on the paper plate. Fasten the brad and spread the feathers. Then color, cut out, and glue the peacock body to the paper plate.

To start their adjective collections, have students brainstorm words that describe peacocks. List the adjectives on the chalkboard for students to copy onto the feathers of their word banks.

Making "Sense" Of Adjectives

This describing activity appeals to the five senses. Each student needs a copy of page 59 and a napkin. Using a hot air popper, pop a batch of popcorn. As the popcorn is popping, have students label their papers, then list adjectives in the proper columns to describe how the popcorn *smells* and *sounds*. Next place a handful of popped corn on each student's napkin and have him list adjectives to describe how the popcorn *looks*, *feels*, and *tastes*. Encourage students to add how-it-*sounds* adjectives to their lists as they munch on the popcorn. As a follow-up writing activity, have students write and illustrate descriptive paragraphs introducing a new brand of popcorn called Papa Peacock's Original Popcorn.

For another sensory experience, provide fresh-baked chocolate chip cookies or minipizzas. Follow-up paragraphs might introduce Mrs. Peacock's Chocolate Chip Delights or Peppy Peacock's Featherweight Pizza.

Kimberly Spring—Gr. 2, Lowell Elementary, Everett, WA

Sizing Up Peacocks

Students can expand their descriptions of *big* and *little* with this "exer-size." As a group, classify each of ten classroom objects as *big* or *little*. Then challenge students to describe the size of each object using more exact adjectives such as *tiny* and *miniature,* or *huge* and *enormous*. List the adjectives on the chalkboard so students can copy them onto the feathers of their word banks. Next have each student write one or more of the adjectives in a sentence that describes a peacock.

jennifer bennett

Feathered Adjectives

How Many?

Adjectives that describe "how many" can add up to fun! On poster board, copy "The Prettiest Peacock" (see illustration). Indicate a word bank at the bottom; then laminate the poster board. Next have students brainstorm adjectives that tell how many. Use a permanent marker to list these adjectives in the word bank. As a large group, complete several versions of the poem by using a wipe-off marker to write the adjectives (and needed articles) on the lines. Read each completed poem in unison before removing the programming with a damp cloth. For added fun, have students recite the poems rap-style!

At the conclusion of the lesson, encourage students to copy adjectives from the word bank onto the feathers of their individual word banks. Later place the poem, writing paper, and student copies of the peacock pattern (page 58) at a center. Have each student copy the poem on writing paper and fill in the blanks. Then have him color a peacock to match.

The Prettiest Peacock

The prettiest peacock I ever knew
Had beautiful feathers! <u>Many</u> feathers were blue.

<u>Numerous</u> feathers were green
And <u>several</u> feathers were red.
There were <u>two</u> orange ones on top of his head!
<u>A few</u> feathers were yellow and bright,
But <u>no</u> feathers were perfectly white!

Word Bank		
few	no	
ten		more
many	numerous	twenty
one hundred	two	most
	several	less

Shades Of…

yellow	red	blue	green	orange	purple	other colors
mustard gold harvest	crimson rose pink fuchsia magenta	navy aqua sapphire turquoise	emerald jade sage	peach melon	burgundy violet plum	gray tan ivory silver

A Fanfare Of Color

Introduce youngsters to an array of descriptive color words. Enlarge the peacock pattern on page 58 onto white bulletin-board paper. Color the peacock's body as desired; then cut out and mount the peacock with the title "A Fanfare Of Color." From the pages of discarded magazines, have students cut circular color samples. Encourage students to look for unusual colors. Then sort and mount the samples atop the peacock's feathers. Next assist students in brainstorming a variety of color names. If possible, point to a sample of each color before listing the color word on a chart such as the one shown. Also make students aware that many colors also name objects (of that color) such as *peach*, *mustard*, and *rose*.

As a follow-up, have students copy several color words from the chart onto the feathers of their word banks.

Prewitt's Spooky Tail

Poor Prewitt the peacock! His tail was nothing more than a few scraggly feathers. Then one day he noticed his tail had grown, and that brought him a new set of problems! Besides being enjoyable, Bill Peet's delightful book *The Spooky Tail Of Prewitt Peacock* (Houghton Mifflin Company, 1979) is a great example of descriptive writing. After reading the story aloud, have students recall the adjectives used to describe Prewitt's tail. Then have students role-play selected story parts, using the adjectives in their dialogues.

Pattern

Use with "A Fanfare Of Color" and
"How Many?" on page 57.

Name _____

Making Sense Of Adjectives

Topic: _____

Sounds...	Feels...	Tastes...	Looks...	Smells...

Note To Teacher: Use with "Making 'Sense' Of Adjectives" on page 56.

Patterns

Use with "Peacock Word Banks" on page 56.

Award

I'm as proud as a peacock of

_____'s

descriptive writing skills!

Teacher _____

Date _____

Hot On The Trail!

In Pursuit Of Parts Of Speech

Get your youngsters on the right track with parts of speech using these trust-worthy ideas from our subscribers. This case may be cracked in record time!

Pam Crane

Love Those Labels

Take an old idea to a new extreme for a parts-of-speech experience your youngsters won't soon forget. After you introduce the concept of nouns, have students label every noun—literally everything—in your classroom. As they work from the obvious nouns (desks, tables, chairs) to ones that may be less obvious (friend, guinea pig, knee, teacher), they'll thoroughly test their knowledge of nouns. It won't be long before students from other classrooms will be asking what the labels are all about—giving your youngsters an opportunity to explain what they know about nouns. Have the students remove the noun labels after they have served their purpose.

Then explain what verbs are, and ask students to label objects with verbs that are associated with them. For example, a pencil may be labeled "writing" or "write" or "writes," and a chalkboard eraser may be labeled "erase" or "erased" or "erasing." Other parts of speech can be examined in much the same way using creative labeling. If this labeling approach really sticks with your students, arrange for students to expand their horizons by similarly labeling the office, the library, or the playground.

Susan K. Brighton—Gr. 2,
Mesa Elementary School, Boulder, CO

Melissa Beasley—Chapter I: Grs. 1-4,
North Columbia Elementary, Appling, GA

The Nouns Are Missing!

Remember Miss Nelson—the one who was missing? As it turns out, she and her substitute teacher, Miss Viola Swamp, may be just the pair you need to teach your youngsters about pronouns. Read aloud *Miss Nelson Is Missing!* by Harry Allard and James Marshall (Houghton Mifflin Company, 1985). Afterward discuss with your students what a substitute teacher is and does. Talk about what *substitute* means. Then explain to your students that pronouns are substitutes for nouns, taking the place of nouns in sentences. Make a chart that features a list of pronouns and a child-drawn likeness of Miss Viola Swamp, the substitute teacher in the story. Write noun-filled sentences on the board and have students substitute pronouns from Miss Swamp's list in place of the nouns in these sentences.

Kathy Horan—Gr. 2, McKinley Intermediate School, Abilene, KS

"Munch" Ado About Adverbs

Looking for a memorable way to introduce adverbs? Then stop at the donut shop on the morning that you plan to bring adverbs to your youngsters' attention, and pick up donut holes. Give each youngster an 8 1/2-inch manila circle, a 3 1/2-inch construction-paper circle, and a brad. Have him center the smaller circle atop the larger one and attach them together in the center with the brad. Then bring out the donut holes and let the munching begin. As students nibble, have them brainstorm verbs that tell what they are doing and adverbs that describe how they are doing it. List the words in two columns on the chalkboard.

When everyone has had his fill, ask each student to imagine that his manila circle is a donut and the circle in the center is the donut hole. Near the center of the donut hole, have him write the word "I." On the donut hole (smaller circle), have him write several of the verbs that have been mentioned. And on the donut (larger circle), have him write several adverbs that describe these verbs. Using crayons, have each youngster "frost" and "decorate" his donut. Then ask each student to use his donut cutout to combine the word "I" with lots of different verb/adverb pairs to create a dozen or more delectable sentences.

Cindy Belote—Gr. 2, Belt Line Elementary, DeSoto, TX

Getting The Hang Of Nouns

This activity makes a neat three-dimensional display and it becomes a handy reference for students, too. Label the front and back of a 36-inch poster-board strip "Nouns"; then label the front and back of each of three 12" x 18" sheets of construction paper with one of the following: "People," "Places," and "Things." Ask students to cut out pictures of people, places, and things from discarded magazines and to glue these cutouts to the fronts or backs of the appropriate construction-paper posters. Laminate the completed posters for durability. Hole-punch four holes in the poster-board strip as shown and one hole at the top of each construction-paper poster. Attach the posters to the strip using lengths of yarn. Then suspend the completed mobile for all to enjoy—and refer to as needed!

Shannon Berry—Gr. 2, Algoma Christian School, Kent City, MI

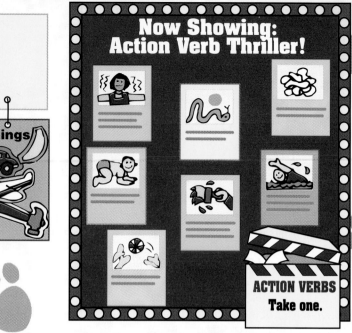

Traces Of Animals And Adjectives

Bring the concept of adjectives to life by having youngsters use adjectives to describe the animals of their choice. Provide a variety of animal stencils. Ask each student to select a stencil, trace it on a sheet of construction paper, and cut it out. On his animal shape, have each student write adjectives that describe the animal. Encourage youngsters to use reference books to find additional adjectives to add to their cutouts. Later use these cutouts to decorate a bulletin board or pages of a student-made book.

VaReane Gray Heese, Omaha, NE

Lights! Camera! Action!

Introduce youngsters to a creative assortment of action verbs at this interactive display. Title a bulletin board "Now Showing: Action Verb Thriller!" and add a border of construction-paper marquee lights as shown. Label numerous paper slips with different action verbs. Place the labeled slips in a box decorated like the one shown. Set the box and a supply of construction paper and half-sheets of drawing paper near the bulletin board.

To complete the activity, a student draws a verb slip from the box and takes the verb, a sheet of construction paper, and a half-sheet of drawing paper to his desk. At his desk he uses crayons or markers to illustrate the verb on the half-sheet of drawing paper. Next he glues his illustration to the construction paper and writes a sentence on the paper that demonstrates proper usage of the verb. After personalizing his work, he attaches it to the bulletin board. This action-packed thriller is a guaranteed blockbuster hit!

Faye Harris Bruce—Gr. 3, Water Valley Elementary, Water Valley, MS

A Big Impression

Are you hoping to make a big impression on your students when you work with them on the parts of speech? Then you're going to think this idea has giant appeal. For one part of speech that your students have covered, cut out giant letters that spell the part-of-speech word. Laminate the letters, if desired, before attaching them to a wall. Have students use permanent markers to write words of that type on the letters. If the laminated letters become too crowded with words, remove the writing with nail polish remover and invite students to find more words to write on the letters. As your students become familiar with other parts of speech, add those oversized words to your walls, too.

Ruth Cobb—Chapter I Reading
Paul Keyes Elementary
Irving, TX

A Wall Of Words

As you introduce a new unit, encourage each student to contribute to a theme-related mural. Once the mural is completed, have youngsters label the nouns on the mural. On the background around the pictures, have youngsters write verbs that relate to the unit and to the nouns on the mural. In the borders of the mural, have youngsters write adjectives that describe the nouns pictured in the mural. As your unit progresses, encourage students to add to the words on the mural and refer to it to add variety to their written assignments.

Tamara Stone—Gr. 3, Mescalero Apache Elementary, Mescalero, NM

Big Book Of Action Verbs

Once youngsters have a clear understanding of action verbs, they'll be eager to show off their parts-of-speech expertise. So why not channel their energies into this big-book project? Assign each child a different alphabet letter, and ask him to come up with an action verb that begins with his assigned letter. Or have students brainstorm the action verbs as a class and have each child choose a different verb from the list. Then have each youngster create a booklet page that features his action verb. To do this, the student writes both the alphabet letter and the chosen verb in large letters. Then he writes and illustrates a sentence that shows the meaning of the verb. Laminate the completed student pages for durability; then compile them in alphabetical order between student-decorated tagboard covers titled "The ABC's Of Action Verbs."

Sara S. Fakoury—Gr. 2
Camden Primary
Camden, SC

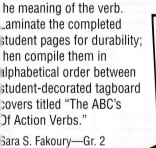

Ll
Listens

My brother listens to music while he brushes his teeth.

Gumshoe Grammar

Students go undercover for this daily parts-of-speech activity! Give each student detective a booklet of blank paper, and have him personalize the booklet covers as desired. Assign the case of the day and have students copy the assignment on a page in their booklets. For example students might copy "The Case Of The Missing Verbs." Then, throughout the day, students jot down brief phrases with the verb actions they observe like "teacher talking" and "principal working." Near the end of the day, either collect and review the booklets, or set aside time for student detectives to share their observations.

Melissa Beasley—Chapter I: Grs. 1–4, North Columbia Elementary, Appling, GA

What's In The Bag?

Keep your youngsters hot on the trail of descriptive adjectives with this homework project. Have each child take home a paper lunch bag labeled with her name. A student chooses one item from home to bring to school in her bag. She writes five adjectives that describe the object on the outside of her bag. Then she places the object inside the bag and staples or tapes the top of the bag closed before transporting her secret cargo to school. The next day at school, each student reads aloud the adjectives on her bag to see if her classmates can identify the mystery object inside. Once her object has been identified (additional clues may need to have been given), the student removes the item from the bag for all to see.

Leigh Anne Newsom—Gr. 3
Greenbrier Intermediate
Chesapeake, VA

soft
tasty
sticky
sweet
crunchy

Maggie

"Betcha" Can't Describe Just One!

Whet your students' appetites for adjectives with this irresistible activity. In advance pour a bag of potato chips into an empty bowl; then glue the empty potato-chip bag to the center of a sheet of poster board. Give each child a paper napkin and two chips. Ask students to eat one chip, concentrating on its taste and texture. Then ask each student to carefully examine her remaining chip. Next have students brainstorm words that describe the chips they ate and studied. Write these descriptive words on the poster-board chart, leaving the top two inches of the chart vacant. When it's appropriate, write "Adjectives" at the top of the chart and explain the meaning of this word. Follow up this activity by having each student write five descriptive sentences about potato chips. While students are completing this portion of the activity, they can munch on a few more chips!

Sara S. Fakoury—Gr. 2, Camden Primary, Camden, SC

Colorful Writing

So you've studied adjectives with your students, but they haven't yet begun to apply their new knowledge to their writing. This idea could be just what you need. After students have completed a writing assignment, have them use their crayons or markers to underline the adjectives they used. Inform students that interesting writing is often described as being *colorful*. Explain that this usage of the word *color* means "full of interest." Ask students to examine their writings and decide if they used enough adjectives to make their writing full of interest or colorful. Have students rewrite their stories, adding a variety of descriptive adjectives. Then have the students once again use markers or crayons to underline the adjectives they used. Now, *that's* colorful writing all the way around!

Roblyn Henry—Gr. 2, Sagebrush Elementary, Aurora, CO

Making All The Right Moves

If you want your lesson on verbs to make a lasting impression, try this idea. Begin with a basic lesson about motion. After a brief explanation, have students brainstorm different methods of movement as you write their ideas on a length of bulletin-board paper. Take your youngsters and the resulting list to an open area such as the school gym or cafeteria. Then have your youngsters act out selected movements from the list. Once you're back in the classroom, challenge the youngsters to identify action verbs in sentences. No doubt they'll find this assignment a snap!

Renee Larsen—Gr. 2, Adams Elementary, Fergus Falls, MN

Adjectives

crunchy
bumpy
tasty
Little Piggy Potato Chips
salty
fried
ripply
greasy

Verb Tense Training

This large-group game is a fun way to reinforce past, present, and future verb tenses with your youngsters. On the chalkboard draw and label a column for each verb tense. Next write a student supply of action verbs on individual cards. Program approximately one-third of these verb cards for each verb tense. Then tape one card to each student's back so that the programming on the card is visible to everyone except the student himself. The object of this game is for each student to tape *his* card in the proper column on the chalkboard. To get his card removed from his back and handed to him by a classmate, a youngster must correctly identify and spell the verb. Students can ask their classmates questions that can be answered with a yes or no, and they can also ask classmates to demonstrate the verbs. When the game is over, have the students check the placement of verbs on the chalkboard and suggest any corrections that need to be made.

LaDawn Rhodes, Shelton Park Elementary, Virginia Beach, VA

Getting A Feel For Adjectives

Here's a hands-on activity that puts students in touch with adjectives. Secretly place a classroom object in a large, paper grocery bag. Set the bag in plain view of your students. Ask a student volunteer to reach inside the bag, feel the object, and use adjectives to describe the object for his classmates. If a student thinks he can identify the mystery object, he raises his hand. When the object has been identified, the volunteer removes the mystery object from the bag for everyone to see; then he trades places with the student who made the correct identification. In the meantime, secretly place another object in the bag. Repeat the activity as often as desired, using a different mystery object each time.

LaDawn Rhodes

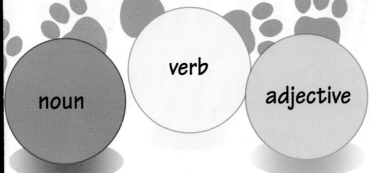

Too Hot To Handle

Does it seem like a little too much to ask that parts of speech could ever become a hot topic among your students? If so, this variation of Hot Potato is just the game for you! Prepare for the game by labeling each of three different-colored balls "noun," "verb," and "adjective," respectively. Have your students sit in a circle, and give the balls to three different participants. Begin a musical recording and ask that students pass the balls quickly around the circle—as if the balls were hot—attempting to be without a ball when the music stops. Unexpectedly stop the music and ask each of the students left holding a ball to name a word that corresponds with the part of speech listed on the ball he holds. Or have the three students who are holding balls supply corresponding words and use these words to make one sentence. If you choose this option, have the other students then identify the noun, verb, and adjective in the sentence given. Start the music again, and watch as interest in parts of speech heats up.

Mary Jo Kampschnieder—Gr. 2, Howells Community Catholic, Howells, NE

Getting Particular About The Parts Of Speech

Once youngsters have learned a few parts of speech, they can apply what they've learned in this activity. Make a large set of word cards for this game, or have each student contribute a few word cards and compile the cards into one big deck. (If your students haven't yet covered all the parts of speech, remove from the deck the cards that belong to categories you haven't yet discussed.) Divide students into small groups and assign each group a different part of speech. Give each group a few of the cards. Then have the members of each group discuss each of the word cards and keep only the ones that match the part of speech they have been assigned. Have each group pass its remaining cards on to another group and repeat the process. Continue having the cards passed in this manner until each group has looked at what's left of each deck. Then have a spokesperson from each group tell about and justify the cards his group kept.

Angela R. Thomas—Gr. 2, Seneca East-Republic Elementary, Republic, OH

Drawing Conclusions About Parts Of Speech

This game plays like a popular game show, but there's a lot of serious learning hidden behind its jovial facade. On separate slips of paper, write dozens of nouns and verbs. Place the slips in a container. To play the game, separate the class into two teams. Have the first person from the first team take a slip from the container, read it, and tell his teammates whether the word is a noun or a verb. Then have him illustrate a clue to the word on the chalkboard. His teammates have three minutes to guess the word. If they guess the word, the team scores a point. If not, no points are earned. Play alternates between the teams. The team with the most points at the end of playing time wins.

Pam Williams—Gr. 3
Dixieland Elementary
Lakeland, FL

The Literature Link

Have you considered looking between the pages of a high-quality children's book for the perfect parts-of-speech activity? The following books are wonderful tools for teaching or reviewing the parts of speech. After sharing a book with your class, have small groups of students create their own books on a part of speech, act out the book as a drama or puppet play, or write another chapter for the book.

Books to use:
Your Foot's On My Feet And Other Tricky Nouns by Marvin Terban
A Cache Of Jewels And Other Collective Nouns by Ruth Heller
Merry-Go-Round: A Book About Nouns by Ruth Heller
Kites Sail High: A Book About Verbs by Ruth Heller
Many Luscious Lollipops: A Book About Adjectives by Ruth Heller
Up, Up And Away: A Book About Adverbs by Ruth Heller
Mine, All Mine!: A Book About Pronouns
Fantastic And Wow!: A Book About Interjections And Conjunctions
Behind The Mask: A Book About Prepositions by Ruth Heller

Awards   Duplicate and present awards to students as desired.

Agent _____

is
hot
on
the
trail
of

_____
_____ .

Keep up the great work!

TOP SECRET!

_____
_____
_____
_____

Congratulations!

What A Super Sleuth!

TOP SECRET

You Cracked The Case!

Agent _____

is
"Top Dog"
when it
comes to

_____
_____
_____ .

Way to go!

Writing Mechanics

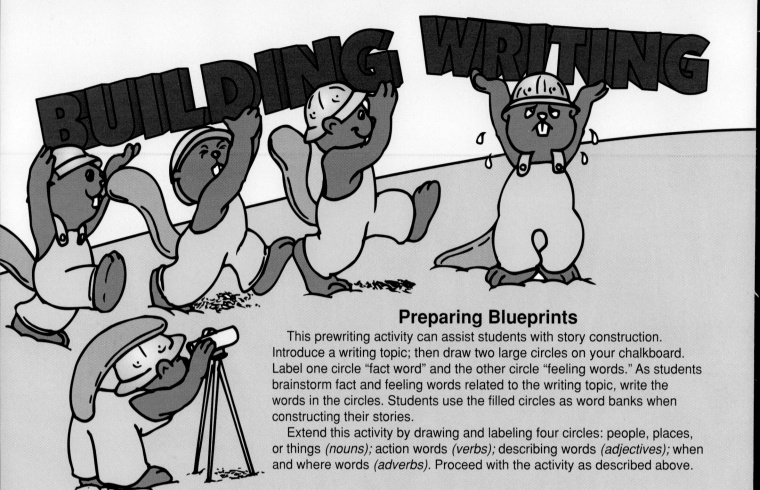

BUILDING WRITING

Preparing Blueprints

This prewriting activity can assist students with story construction. Introduce a writing topic; then draw two large circles on your chalkboard. Label one circle "fact word" and the other circle "feeling words." As students brainstorm fact and feeling words related to the writing topic, write the words in the circles. Students use the filled circles as word banks when constructing their stories.

Extend this activity by drawing and labeling four circles: people, places, or things *(nouns);* action words *(verbs);* describing words *(adjectives);* when and where words *(adverbs).* Proceed with the activity as described above.

The Writer's Toolbox

This story structure activity will have your crew writing stories in a snap! Write each sentence of a three-sentence story on a separate sheet of paper. Label the backs of the sheets "beginning," "middle," or "ending" to correspond with the story sequence. Place the sheets inside a toolbox.

Present your writer's toolbox to students, explaining that the toolbox contains three necessary tools for story construction. Unveil the tools separately, examining the fronts and backs of the sheets. With student assistance, turn these "tools" into a story.

Assist students as they construct stories of their own. Have each student fold a large sheet of story paper into thirds (as shown), then cut on the folds to create three sheets of story paper. Label the backs of the sheets to match those in the toolbox; then provide time for students to construct their stories. Finished stories can be stapled together.

A Writer's Checklist

Experienced writers can benefit from a writer's checklist such as the one on page 70. Duplicate and distribute student copies, instructing students to check off each guideline as they evaluate their writing. This writing step would precede the proofing step and eliminate careless mistakes. The checklist may be expanded to fit the needs of your writers.

Beginning Builders

Young writers can find writing success with rebus stories. Begin building around simple vocabulary words such as *a, the, is,* and *has.* Encourage writers to draw rebus pictures or use inventive spellings for unknown words. This writing process removes the anxiety that is often associated with writing. The stories may then be illustrated and shared if desired. Challenge older writers to use rebus pictures to replace the nouns or verbs in their stories.

SKILLS

It's time to roll up your sleeves and begin building writing skills! You'll find easy-to-follow blueprints for a successful writing program along with reproducibles, awards, and a ready-to-use activity center on the following pages. You've won the bid on this building contract!

by Mary Anne Haffner and Sue Ireland

The Final Touches

Proofreading, or adding the final touches, is a step that can be taken at any grade level. Duplicate and distribute student copies of "The Final Touches" on page 70. With student assistance, display and proof three-sentence stories. Provide further proofing practice by duplicating three-sentence stories for students to proof independently, then check together. Provide colored pencils or fine-tip markers for students to use when they begin proofing their own stories.

Students can also work as editing partners. After a student has edited his partner's work, he writes a note to his partner that includes a positive sentence about the story and one writing suggestion (if applicable). The partners may then work together to correct spelling and punctuation errors.

Tools Of The Trade

Give student writers access to a variety of writing tools by setting up a permanent "Writers' Corner" in your classroom. Gather a thesaurus, a pictionary, a dictionary, alphabet stamps, a proofreading chart, a writer's checklist, an old typewriter, and a variety of writing paper to place in this special area. And, of course, you'll need a toolbox for storing items such as markers, crayons, pencils, erasers, and stickers! Encourage writers to visit this area at their leisure. If possible, designate an area near your "Writers' Corner" for displaying student stories year-round. Along with providing a special writing area, you'll be providing terrific writing motivation!

Writing Exhibits

Showcasing your writers' completed work in a variety of ways will bring rave reviews! These suggestions require a minimal amount of preparation:

— Place stories (complete with title pages) in clear plastic report covers. Display stories in your room or school library.

— Copy the stories of young writers onto chart paper (using colorful markers); then mount on poster board and laminate. Display stories independently or create a big book of stories by binding the laminated stories together with metal rings.

— Schedule times for writers to share stories with students in other classrooms.

— Ask your librarian to host a "Meet The Authors Day." A videotape presentation can feature interviews of student writers (informing others about why they enjoy writing, how they think of ideas, or writing tips) and a sampling of their works.

Patterns And Certificate

Use the patterns with "A Writer's Checklist" on page 68 and "The Final Touches" on page 69.

Name _____

My Writing Checklist

_____ Each sentence begins with a capital letter.

_____ Each sentence ends with a **.** or **?** or **!**.

_____ The first sentence of my story is indented.

_____ All misspelled words are corrected.

Congratulations!

_____
Student

for becoming a
Master Craftsman
of process writing!

_____
Job Site Foreman

_____
Date

The Final Touches!

Proofing symbols:

≡ = **capital letter is needed**

— = **lowercase letter is needed**

℮ = **take this out**

∧ = **add this**

◯ = **check the spelling**

be soore to proof your be Writing carefully.

Name _____

Open _____

Writing Tools

Note To Teacher: Duplicate this sheet. Have students write word banks for writing topics in their toolboxes. Or program the sheet with words for writing topics before duplicating.

A Classic Tale Of Punctuation

If you're looking for a happy ending, try this unique approach to practicing punctuation. Using familiar folklore characters, we've spun a tale of ending punctuation practice with magical appeal!

ideas contributed by Mary Anne Haffner & Sue Ireland

Magical Appeal

Add to the magical appeal of this collection of activities and reproducibles by giving each youngster a dose of punctuation power! To do this, attach a magical flag to the top of each student's pencil as shown. (Use a glitter pen to decorate the masking-tape flag.) Encourage students to use their pencils for all writing assignments. Of course the pencils aren't magic, but the sparkling reminder attached to the pencil will help youngsters remember to check their writing for ending punctuation. To enhance the magical mood, occasionally sprinkle the top of a bookshelf, desktop, or chalkboard tray with glitter or party confetti (available in assorted colors and shapes in the party sections of most card shops). It's a great way to recognize your youngsters' punctuation efforts.

Golly, Goldilocks!

Does anyone know why Goldilocks entered the home of the three bears uninvited? Your youngsters may have some ideas! After reviewing the tale of Goldilocks and the Three Bears, have each youngster list the names of the four story characters on his paper. Then, below each name, have him write a question that he would like to ask that character. Next have each youngster trade papers with a classmate. Each student then checks the punctuation of his partner's written questions. If the punctuation is correct, he writes a response to each of the questions (ending each response with either a period or an exclamation point). If the questions are punctuated incorrectly, he returns them (unanswered) to his partner and asks him to make the necessary changes. Each pair of students keeps working together until each partner has a correctly punctuated answer for each of his correctly punctuated questions.

Breaking The Spell

After reading aloud a favorite version of *Beauty And The Beast,* your youngsters will be eager to break a spell themselves. Display several incorrectly punctuated sentences related to the story. Inform students that you have placed a punctuation spell over the sentences. Then challenge each youngster to break the spell by copying the sentences on his paper and replacing all incorrect punctuation marks with correct ones. When a youngster breaks the spell, mount his paper on a display titled "From Beastly To Beautiful!" Repeat the activity for each of several days using different sets of sentences related to the story. Who knows? Students may fall in love with punctuation practice!

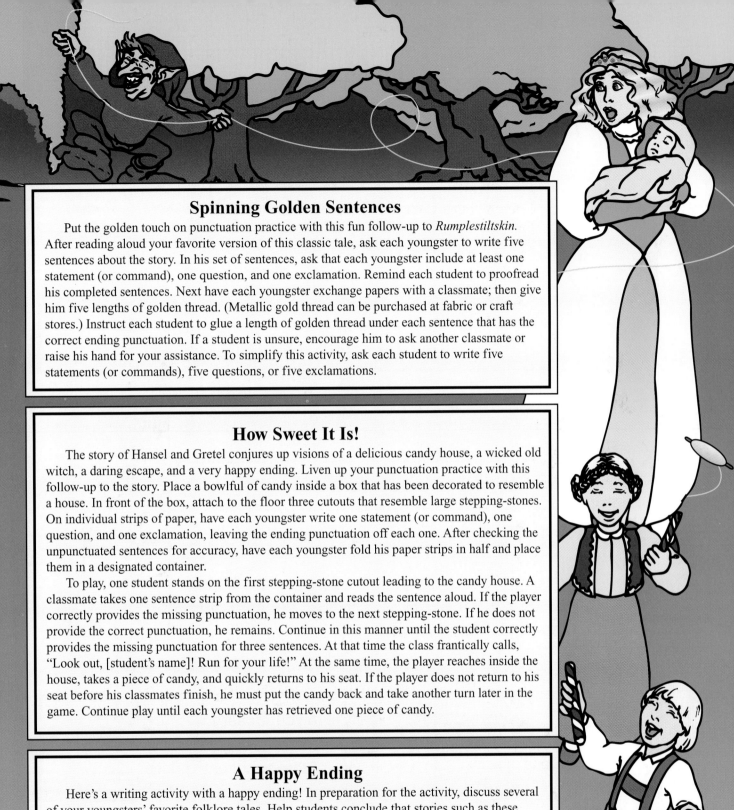

Spinning Golden Sentences

Put the golden touch on punctuation practice with this fun follow-up to *Rumplestiltskin*. After reading aloud your favorite version of this classic tale, ask each youngster to write five sentences about the story. In his set of sentences, ask that each youngster include at least one statement (or command), one question, and one exclamation. Remind each student to proofread his completed sentences. Next have each youngster exchange papers with a classmate; then give him five lengths of golden thread. (Metallic gold thread can be purchased at fabric or craft stores.) Instruct each student to glue a length of golden thread under each sentence that has the correct ending punctuation. If a student is unsure, encourage him to ask another classmate or raise his hand for your assistance. To simplify this activity, ask each student to write five statements (or commands), five questions, or five exclamations.

How Sweet It Is!

The story of Hansel and Gretel conjures up visions of a delicious candy house, a wicked old witch, a daring escape, and a very happy ending. Liven up your punctuation practice with this follow-up to the story. Place a bowlful of candy inside a box that has been decorated to resemble a house. In front of the box, attach to the floor three cutouts that resemble large stepping-stones. On individual strips of paper, have each youngster write one statement (or command), one question, and one exclamation, leaving the ending punctuation off each one. After checking the unpunctuated sentences for accuracy, have each youngster fold his paper strips in half and place them in a designated container.

To play, one student stands on the first stepping-stone cutout leading to the candy house. A classmate takes one sentence strip from the container and reads the sentence aloud. If the player correctly provides the missing punctuation, he moves to the next stepping-stone. If he does not provide the correct punctuation, he remains. Continue in this manner until the student correctly provides the missing punctuation for three sentences. At that time the class frantically calls, "Look out, [student's name]! Run for your life!" At the same time, the player reaches inside the house, takes a piece of candy, and quickly returns to his seat. If the player does not return to his seat before his classmates finish, he must put the candy back and take another turn later in the game. Continue play until each youngster has retrieved one piece of candy.

A Happy Ending

Here's a writing activity with a happy ending! In preparation for the activity, discuss several of your youngsters' favorite folklore tales. Help students conclude that stories such as these routinely have happy endings. Then choose one tale, and challenge your students to brainstorm other possible endings for the story—happy endings, of course. Next have each youngster write and illustrate a new ending for the chosen classic. Ask that each youngster include at least one statement, one question, and one exclamation in his story. When the stories are written, pair students and have each youngster read his story aloud to his partner. Then, working together, have each twosome check their papers for complete sentences and correct ending punctuation. Circulate among the working pairs, adding sparkling comments to their papers (using a glitter pen) or dusting their desks with tiny sprinkles of confetti.

True Love

Follow the directions for each sentence group.

Add a **period (.)** at the end of each sentence that makes a statement. Draw a blue line through each of the other sentences.	1. The Beast lived in a beautiful palace
	2. He was very kind to Beauty
	3. Could Beauty ever love the Beast
	4. Oh, please marry me
	5. The Beast had a very sad heart

Add a **question mark (?)** at the end of each sentence that asks something. Draw a green line through each of the other sentences.	6. Is Beauty frightened of the Beast
	7. Listen to the beautiful music
	8. Beauty missed her father
	9. Will Beauty return to the palace of the Beast
	10. Does Beauty love the Beast

Add a **exclamation point (!)** at the end of each sentence that shows surprise or strong feeling. Draw a red line through each of the other sentences.	11. I really love you, Beast
	12. Oh, look at that handsome prince
	13. Wasn't the wedding beautiful
	14. Wow, they look happy
	15. Beauty and the Prince lived happily ever after

Bonus Box: On the back of this sheet, write three sentences about someone you love.

©1998 The Education Center, Inc. • *The Best Of* THE MAILBOX® *Language Arts* • Primary • TEC1459 • Key p. 160

Name _____

Punctuation Porridge

Read each sentence.
Add the missing punctuation.
Cross out the same mark on a bowl of porridge below.

1. Three bears lived in a house in the woods

2. Goldilocks took a walk in the woods

3. Why did Goldilocks walk into the bears' home

4. Each of the three bears had a bowl for porridge

5. Wow, that porridge is hot

6. Oh no, the chair broke

7. Should Goldilocks go upstairs

8. What a huge bed

9. Goldilocks fell fast asleep in Baby Bear's bed

10. The three bears came home

11. Who has been eating my porridge

12. Who broke Baby Bear's chair

13. Look who is in my bed

14. Will the bears ever see Goldilocks again

Bonus Box: Check the porridge bowls. Papa Bear should have three **periods** left. Mama Bear should have 2 **question marks** left, and Baby Bear should have only one **exclamation point** left. How well did you do?

Spinning Golden Sentences

If a sentence has correct punctuation,
color the spool of thread gold.
If a sentence has incorrect punctuation,
turn the sentence into straw by drawing a yellow line through it.

1. A man told the king that his daughter could spin straw into gold?

2. The girl was sent to the king.

3. Could the girl spin straw into gold!

4. Who was this tiny man?

5. Oh, please help me!

6. The tiny man spun the straw into gold?

7. Will the tiny man return.

8. What gift will the tiny man receive tonight?

9. Please, not my firstborn child.

10. Could the girl learn the man's name in three days?

11. Was his name Stringbones.

12. His name was not Phil.

13. Could the man's name be Rumpelstiltskin?

14. The tiny man left the room in a fury?

15. Look at him go!

 ©1998 The Education Center, Inc. • *The Best Of* THE MAILBOX® *Language Arts* • *Primary* • TEC1459 • Key p. 160

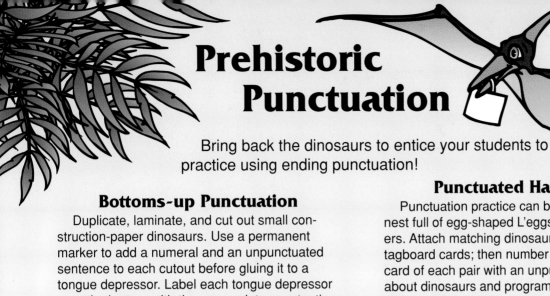

Prehistoric Punctuation

Bring back the dinosaurs to entice your students to practice using ending punctuation!

Bottoms-up Punctuation

Duplicate, laminate, and cut out small construction-paper dinosaurs. Use a permanent marker to add a numeral and an unpunctuated sentence to each cutout before gluing it to a tongue depressor. Label each tongue depressor near the bottom with the appropriate punctuation. Stand these dinosaurs in a sand-filled box.

Students number their pages, copy and punctuate the sentences, and lift each dinosaur to check. For variety, remove the original sentences with rubbing alcohol and reprogram using a permanent marker.

"Question-asaurus"

"Question-asaurus" serves as an ever-present reminder of the words that are likely to appear at the beginning of asking sentences. Enlarge a simple dinosaur outline on bulletin-board paper, cut out, and attach to an unoccupied wall. Whenever you introduce a new "asking word," have a student write that word on the dinosaur cutout.

Duplicate several copies of the same dinosaur outline and place them in a center. In their free time, students may use the words from the large dinosaur cutout to compose asking sentences on the small dinosaur copies. Students may display their dinosaurs near "Question-asaurus."

Punctuated Hatchlings

Punctuation practice can be hatched from a nest full of egg-shaped L'eggs® hosiery containers. Attach matching dinosaur stickers to pairs of tagboard cards; then number and program one card of each pair with an unpunctuated question about dinosaurs and program the other with the same number and the corresponding unpunctuated answer. Store each card pair inside a numbered plastic egg, and nestle the egg in a box of packing chips. To play, a student opens one egg at a time, determines which sentence is *asking* and which is *telling,* and copies and punctuates first the question and then the answer on his own paper.

Punctuation Alert

Have students emphasize the ending punctuation while copying sentences about dinosaurs. Provide a red ink pad and a dinosaur stamp. Each student will also need paper, a pencil, and a green crayon. Because green means go, have students write the first letter of each sentence with a green crayon. Because red means stop, have students stamp a red dinosaur at the end of each sentence and write the appropriate punctuation on the dinosaur.

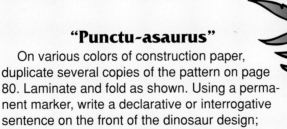

"Punctu-asaurus"

On various colors of construction paper, duplicate several copies of the pattern on page 80. Laminate and fold as shown. Using a permanent marker, write a declarative or interrogative sentence on the front of the dinosaur design; then write the corresponding punctuation inside the fold. Students write and punctuate each sentence before unfolding the dinosaur design to check their answers.

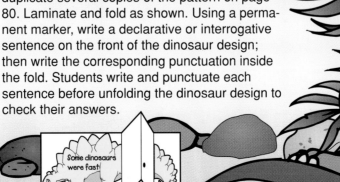

"Dino-riffic" Punctuation

Perk up punctuation practice with this playful activity. Prepare a set of unpunctuated sentence cards. Divide students into two teams and have the teams sit in parallel lines on the floor. Place an empty basket in front of the teams and a basket behind the teams containing two balls labeled with periods and two balls labeled with question marks.

To play, the leader of each line comes up to the empty basket, where you show both of them an unpunctuated sentence card. Both students read the card silently and return to their seats in line, where they whisper to the people behind them, "Period" or "Question mark," to indicate the punctuation needed to finish the sentence. The type of punctuation is whispered down each line of students until it reaches the last person in each line, who runs to the basket, chooses a ball with the requested punctuation, and takes it to his place. Team members pass the ball to the front of the line. The leader carries the ball to the basket and has a seat at the end of the line. A correct response scores one point for the team. Award the winning team with dinosaur stickers if desired.

To extend this learning experience, write each punctuated sentence on the board during the game; then have students read and discuss the punctuation. At the end of the game, erase the punctuation from the end of each sentence, and have students copy and punctuate the sentences.

Name_____Open

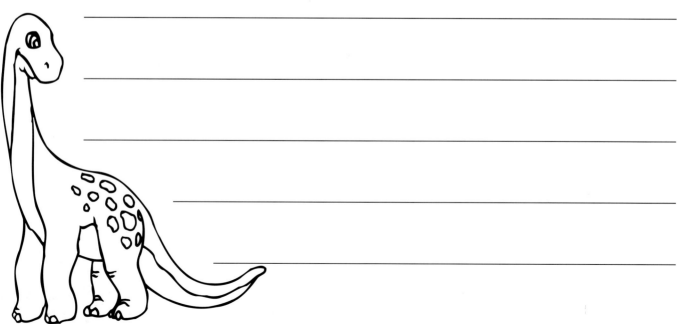

"Dino-mite" Punctuation

Cut on the slits. Paste two squares on the back of this page to cover the slits.
Cut apart each sentence. Place each sentence in a pocket.

Asking Sentences ?

slit

Telling Sentences •

slit

Bonus Box: Match each asking sentence to the telling sentence that answers it.

©1998 The Education Center, Inc. • *The Best Of* THE MAILBOX® *Language Arts* • *Primary* • TEC1459 • Key p. 160

Were all dinosaurs big	Maybe it got too cold for them
Some dinosaurs were little	How do we know about dinosaurs
What does dinosaur mean	Most are plants
How often did dinosaurs eat	What did dinosaurs like to eat
It means terrible lizard	What made dinosaurs die out
Bones and tracks were found	Some dinosaurs ate all day long

Note To Teacher: Provide two 3" x 3" squares for each student to paste to the back of his paper, covering the slits.

79

Patterns

Use with "Punctu-asaurus" on page 77.

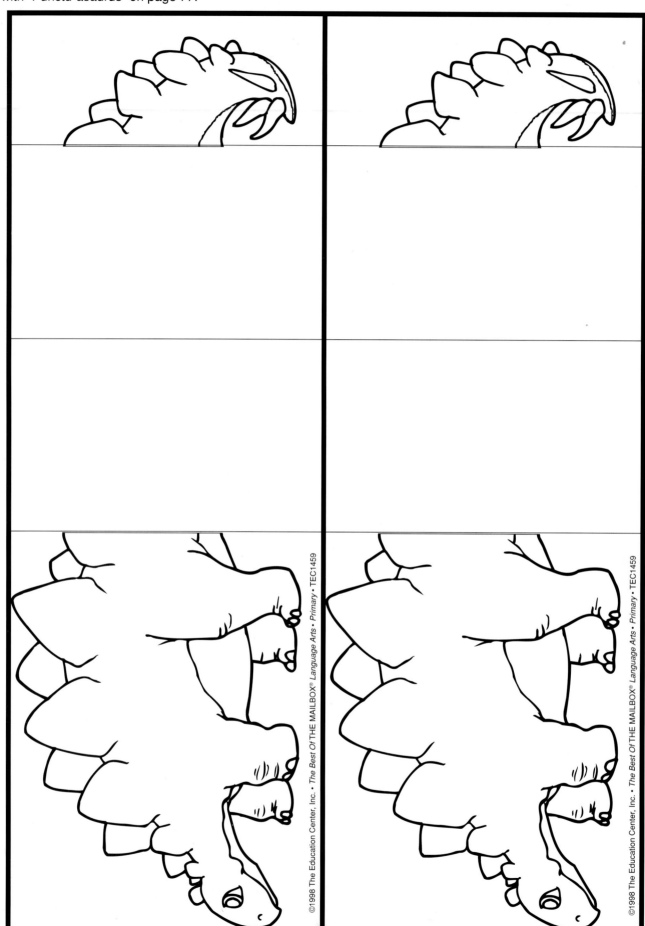

Swing Into Editing

There's no monkey business in this unit—just practical, classroom-tested ideas for improving students' editing skills. So choose your favorites and go bananas! Editing will be more fun than a barrel of monkeys!

The Daily Edit

Boost students' editing expertise with daily editing practice. Before students arrive each day, write a sentence that contains spelling, punctuation, and/or capitalization errors on the chalkboard. Edit the sentence with your students; then have each student rewrite the sentence correctly in a personalized editing notebook.

Read-Aloud Editing

Improve students' editing skills with this sound tip! Each time a student finishes a writing assignment, have him take his paper and pencil to a special read-aloud area. Then have him read his work aloud, stopping to correct any mistakes he finds. Using this method, writing errors and missing words can be discovered quickly.

Wipe-Off Editing

This editing method clearly builds writing confidence. When working with individual students, clip a clear sheet of acetate atop a student's paper before beginning the editing process. As you edit the paper with the student, have him use a wipe-off pen to mark all corrections on the acetate. Next instruct the student to write his final draft by referring to his edited work. When his final draft is complete, he can remove the acetate and wipe it clean with a damp sponge. Without editing marks, the student's original draft remains intact, as does his self-confidence!

Editing Table

An editing table is the perfect work area for budding writers. To set up an editing table, tape several laminated editing checklists atop a tabletop. Then place a few dictionaries, junior thesauruses, and/or word lists on the table, along with a supply of colored pens or pencils. Encourage each student to edit his own work at the editing table before scheduling a writer's conference.

Editing Buddies

Editing buddies can help students learn the editing process. Pair each of your students with an editing buddy from an intermediate grade. When a student has a rough draft to edit, his editing buddy can assist him in finding and correcting spelling, capitalization, and punctuation errors. This system gives your students one-on-one editing experience, and it provides intermediate students with additional editing practice, too.

Barry Slate

The Sentence Monitor

Use this proven method to help beginning writers make sense of sentences. Duplicate a supply of editing forms such as the one shown. After writing each sentence of his rough draft, a student checks his sentence against his editing form. He then checks off each item after making any necessary adjustments to the sentence. When he has written and edited five sentences, help the student edit his writing for spelling errors.

Team Editing

A team effort makes editing easier. Divide students into teams. Assign each team a pen color and an editing task (for example, blue/capitalization, red/spelling, green/punctuation). Then give each team several rough drafts. The members of each team work together to find errors in their assigned category. All proofreading marks are made in the appropriate pen color. When a rough draft has been edited, it is passed on to another team. Continue in this manner until all teams have edited each rough draft. Routinely change the teams' tasks so that all students can experience editing different types of errors.

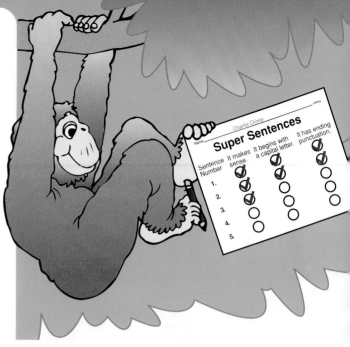

Peer Editing

Editing a peer's work is a great way for students to practice proofreading skills. After writing rough drafts, pair students. Each student edits his partner's draft for proper spelling, capitalization, and punctuation. He then writes his name at the top of the paper. The writer makes the corrections to his rough draft before having a final editing session with the teacher. This method gives students a chance to polish their papers before conferencing with the teacher.

Proofreading "A-peel"

These special proofreading forms have a lot of "a-peel." Duplicate student copies of the proofreading form on page 84. During an individual writing conference, have each student read his rough draft to you. Then have him read it aloud a second time as you assist him in finding three misspelled words. Write the words correctly on a copy of the form; then have the student write each word on a banana. (If desired, the student can add these words to his personal word list.) Next assist the student in finding two sentences that have punctuation and/or capitalization errors. With your help, have the student write the sentences correctly on his form. Staple the completed form to the rough draft. Students gain an awareness about editing without the confusion of editing marks or the frustration of recopying their papers.

Punctuation Edit

This hands-on activity makes editing for punctuation marks "rice" and easy. In advance, use food coloring to tint rice red, blue, green, and yellow. After writing a rough draft, have each student glue a piece of rice atop each punctuation mark according to the code. Piece by piece, students' awareness of proper punctuation will grow.

Punctuation Code		
red	=	period
blue	=	comma
green	=	question mark
yellow	=	exclamation mark

Computer-Paper Drafts

Computer paper provides the perfect format for writing rough drafts. Have students write their rough drafts on the white spaces, leaving the colored spaces blank. When it's time to edit, students have plenty of room to make corrections in the colored spaces. If the sentence order needs adjusting, it can easily be changed by cutting and pasting. Be sure to recycle the computer paper after the final drafts are written!

Editing Manipulatives

Take a hands-on approach to editing with editing cards. For each student, program a set of four cards with a period, a question mark, an exclamation mark, and a capital *C*. Laminate the cards for durability; then store each set in a resealable plastic bag. Before students edit their work, distribute the bags. Have each child remove the period card from his bag, then check his paper for proper use of periods. Repeat the procedure for question marks, exclamation marks, and capital letters. At the end of the editing session, collect the bags of cards and store them for later use.

Writing Workshop Groups

In a workshop group, the input from other group members helps each student fine-tune his writing. Divide students into small groups; then have students share their writing with group members during each step of the writing process. During the editing step, have group members read one another's rough drafts and make oral and/or written comments. After the group edit, a student either writes his final draft or schedules a final editing conference with the teacher.

Monkeying Around With Editing

Mold better editing skills with a little monkey business. As students watch, sculpt a slightly imperfect monkey from clay. When the sculpture is complete, have students critique your work. Then have students make suggestions for improvement like moving the ears, lengthening the tail, or making the head smaller. Then tell students that good writers also "sculpt" their writing by moving words around and adding or taking away words. Finally, have student pairs work together to sculpt their own rough drafts. Encourage students to share the improved versions with their classmates.

Chimp's Checklist

Students will swing into editing with this chimp's handy checklist! Duplicate student copies of the checklist on page 84. Have each student attach a copy of the checklist to his rough draft, then evaluate his writing using the checklist criteria. You'll flip over your students' improved editing skills!

Our thanks to the following contributors:
Judy Armstrong—Gr. 2, Rib Mt. School, Wausau, WI; **Laura Blevins**—Gr. 3, Wright Elementary School, Wright, KS; **Maggie Diaz**—Gr. 2, Poinciana Elementary, Naples, FL; **Joyce Erickson**—Resource Room, Wisner Elementary School, Wisner, NE; **Arlene Haynes**—Gr. 2, Oak Valley Elementary, Omaha, NE; **Karen Hohner**—Grs. 1 and 2, Manning Elementary, Alberta, Canada; **Kathy Howley**—Gr. 1, Hayshire Elementary School, York, PA; **Patricia Judd**—Gr. 3, Sandy, UT; **Donna Lemorrocco**—Gr. 2, Val Vista Lakes Elementary, Gilbert, AZ; **Norina Nicholson**—Gr. 2, Our Lady Of The Assumption, Toronto, Ontario, Canada; **Gina Parisi**—Gr. 2, Demarest School, Bloomfield, NJ; **Melody Parsons**, Crossroads Elementary, Whitwell, TN; **Denise Quinn**—Gr. 1, Mill Lake School, Spotswood, NJ; **Pam Straub**—Gr. 2, Trinity Lutheran School, Janesville, MN; **Pamela Williams**—Gr. 3, Dixieland Elementary, Lakeland, FL

Name ________________________________ Proofreading

Proofreading "A-peel"

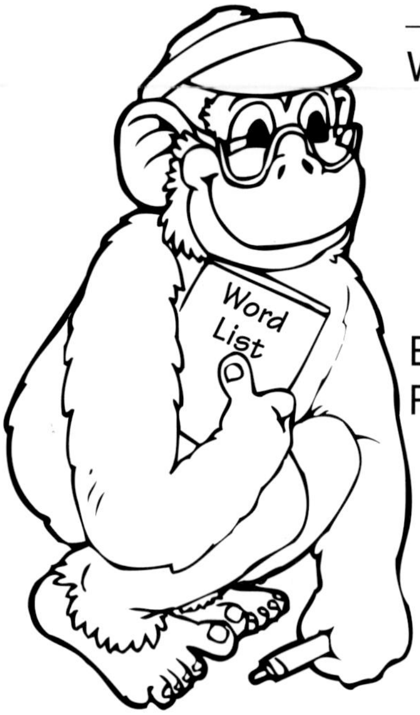

Learn to spell these words: ______________________

____

Write the words on the bananas.

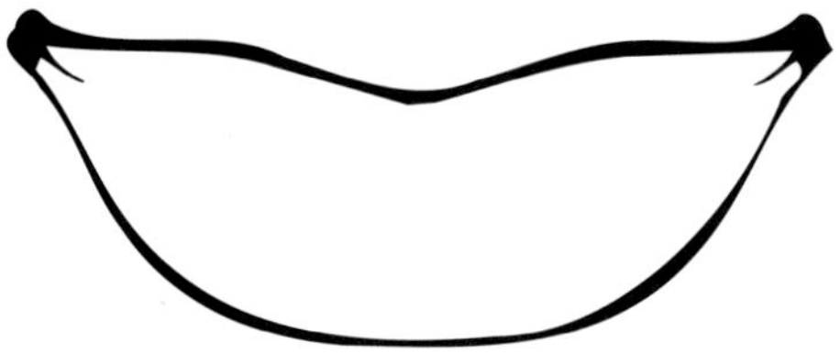

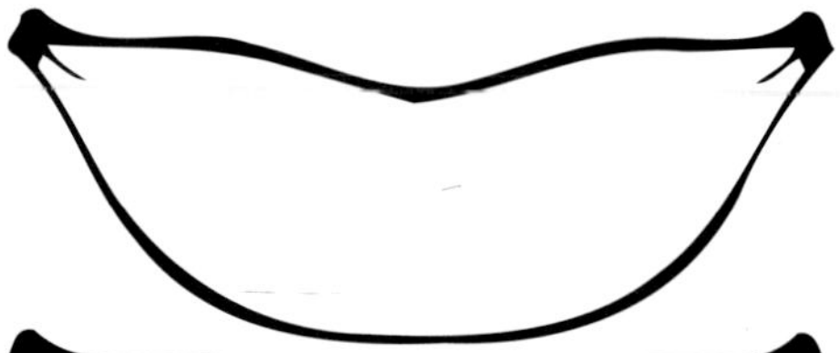

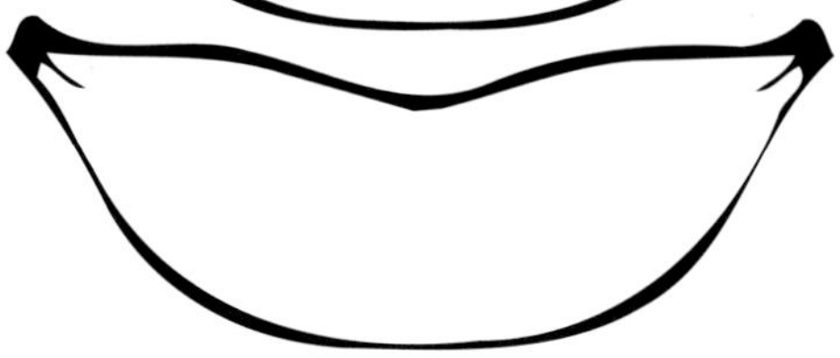

Edit two sentences.
Rewrite them on the lines below.

1. ______________________

____

2. ______________________

____

Name ________________________________ Editing

Chimp's Checklist

Read each question.
Edit your work.
Check the answer.

	Yes	No
Capitalization Did you capitalize the first word of each sentence?	☐	☐
Handwriting Did you write neatly?	☐	☐
Indentation Did you indent the first line of each paragraph?	☐	☐
Margins Did you keep the margins straight?	☐	☐
Punctuation Did you put a **.**, **?**, or **!** at the end of each sentence?	☐	☐
Spelling Did you check your spelling?	☐	☐

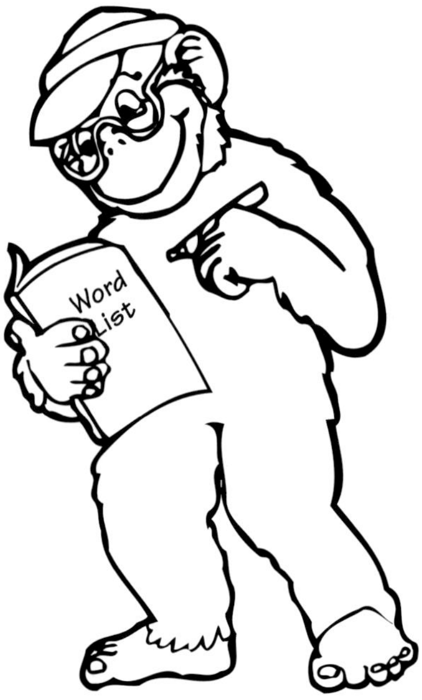

 Note To Teacher: Use the first reproducible with "Proofreading 'A-peel' " on page 82. Use the second reproducible with "Chimp's Checklist" on page 83.

Writing And Publishing

Getting Started On The "Write" Foot!

Step "write" up to this collection of easy-to-implement writing activities! Your students' writing skills will be in business in no time—and there's no fancy footwork involved!

ideas by Lisa Kelly

The "Write" Foot

Get your students started on the "write" foot with these colorful student-made journals. Use the footprint pattern on page 90 to duplicate a class supply of journal covers. Place the journal covers, 9" x 12" sheets of construction paper, a supply of 4" x 8" writing paper, scissors, and a stapler at a center. To make her journal, a student personalizes and cuts out a journal cover. Next she positions the cutout atop a sheet of construction paper, traces around the shape, and cuts on the resulting outline. Then she staples a supply of writing paper between her two journal covers. Continually keep this center stocked with journal-making supplies so that students can create additional journals as needed. If desired, set aside time each day for students to write in their " 'Write' Foot" journals. See "Staying In Step" on page 89 for how to use the foot character as a daily writing prompt.

The "Write" Foot!

Name Maggie

All About Me

An oral reading of *Clive Eats Alligators* by Alison Lester (Houghton Mifflin Company, 1991) is the perfect prewriting activity for an "All About Me" booklet project. The seven characters in this book delightfully model diversity with their varying interests and preferences. At the conclusion of the book, list the eight featured subtitles on the chalkboard. Then give each child a construction-paper booklet containing eight blank booklet pages. Have each child write her name and the title "All About Me" on the front booklet cover, then copy a different subtitle near the top of each booklet page. To complete her booklet, a student writes and illustrates a sentence that describes her personal preference or interest about each featured subtitle. Set aside time each day for several students to share their completed projects with their classmates. If you can find the time, complete and share a booklet about yourself, too. Students will enjoy learning about their classmates and their teacher, and you'll quickly learn a lot about your class!

Shopping

I like to visit the pet store.

Colorful Counting

Not only can you count on this ten-day journal activity to review number words and color words—it also strengthens question-and-answer skills! Under your students' direction, write the number words from one through ten on a length of bulletin-board paper. In a similar manner, create a list of color words. Post the resulting lists for student reference. Give each child a construction-paper journal that holds ten sheets of story paper. Have each student write her name and the title "Colorful Counting" on the front cover of her journal, then add other desired cover artwork.

To begin the journal activity, write "How many _____?" on the chalkboard. Exhibit one item and ask a student volunteer to orally complete the question. Then ask another volunteer to answer the question, stipulating that the answer must include a number word and a color word. Write the student's answer on the chalkboard. Repeat this procedure several times, using a different item each time. Then ask each student to write, answer, and illustrate the modeled question in her journal. Over the next nine school days, spotlight the numbers two through ten in sequential order. In a few days, the students will be eager to identify their own number sets, allowing you to omit this step in the procedure. Later in the year, repeat the activity—this time relating it to the current theme of study. "How many sloths in the rain forest?"

How many apples?

There are three red apples.

Happy

I was happy on my birthday!

Exploring Emotions

Sometimes youngsters have difficulty identifying the emotions they're feeling. This journal activity invites students to explore and better understand their feelings.

Each child needs a construction-paper journal that contains five or more blank pages. Ask each student to title the front cover of his journal "My Feelings," then personalize it with his name and other desired decorations. To complete a journal entry, introduce an emotion like happy, sad, calm, surprised, or angry. Write the emotion on the chalkboard and demonstrate facial expressions and body language that portray the emotion. Encourage students to talk about times they've experienced this feeling. Next have each child write the emotion at the top of a blank journal page and illustrate a time when he felt this way. Students may also write (or dictate for you to write) about their experiences. Explore a different emotion every few days. When the journals are completed, ask students to continue to store them in their desks. The completed journals can be handy tools for the students (and yourself) when interpersonal conflicts arise.

Handfuls Of Achievements!

This weekly writing activity creates a handy year-round display! Each week ask every student to trace the outline of his hand onto colored paper and cut out the resulting shape. Inside the hand cutout, have the child write his name and one accomplishment from the past school week. After each child has shared his accomplishment with the class, display the students' handiwork on a bulletin board titled "Give Us A Hand!" At the end of each month or grading period, ask your students to join you in applauding the entire class for its outstanding accomplishments. Then remove the hand cutouts from the display and send them home with the students so that the accomplishments can be shared with family members.

I scored 100% on my math test!

Ricki Almo

A Family Affair

Students will find writing about their family members an enjoyable task. And because this writing activity results in a one-of-a-kind project, the task is even more desirable! Each student needs a white construction-paper copy of the paper-doll pattern (on page 91) for each family member, including himself. On each pattern—in the provided box—a student names and describes a different family member. Then the student cuts out and decorates his patterns to resemble his family members. Provide an assortment of arts-and-crafts supplies for decorating that includes crayons; yarn; buttons; and scraps of fabric, construction paper, and wallpaper. Remind students not to decorate over their writing. To assemble his family booklet, a student arranges his decorated cutouts side by side in a desired order. Then, working from left to right, he glues each tab to the adjoining cutout. The student trims off the final tab and his project is complete. Have the students form a sharing circle so that each youngster may introduce his family of cutouts to his classmates. If you're preparing for Open House, be sure to display these one-of-a-kind family projects for your visitors to enjoy!

What A Walk!

I Went Walking, written by Sue Williams and illustrated by Julie Vivas (Harcourt Brace Jovanovich, Publishers; 1996), is a perfect springboard for a beginning-of-the-year writing activity. This easy-to-read picture book chronicles the colorful critters that a small boy encounters while on an innocent stroll.

For an independent writing activity, have each student copy the sentences "I went walking" and "What did I see?" near the top of a 9" x 12" sheet of drawing paper. Instruct each child to illustrate her paper by drawing herself and part of the animal she plans to see. Suggest that the students picture themselves (and the partially hidden animals) in the animals' natural surroundings. Next have each student copy, complete, and illustrate the sentence "I saw a [color] [animal] looking at me" on the back of her paper. Assemble the students' work into a class book titled "We Went Walking." No doubt your students will take a walk to the classroom library to check out this class publication!

If you prefer to follow up your oral reading of *I Went Walking* with a group activity, try this! For each group you will need a length of white paper labeled with the sentences "We went walking" and "What did we see?" As a class, brainstorm places that the students would like to walk, such as a beach, a city, a forest, and a jungle. List the students' ideas on the chalkboard. Next divide the class into groups. After each group has chosen a different place to take its walk, distribute the lengths of paper that you've programmed. Ask the members of each group to use crayons or markers to illustrate their length of paper to show the things they imagine seeing on their walk. Display the resulting artwork for all to see. Older students can write the name of each illustrated item on a blank index card, then tape the cards to their group's artwork near the corresponding illustrations.

A hospital in Edina, MN, is where I was born on May 17, 1989.

Beautiful is the word my parents used to describe me.

Alphabet Autobiographies

Teach your students the ABCs of writing autobiographies with this unique approach. At home, have each student research special events from his life; then have him bring his findings to school. On separate sheets of paper, ask each child to write autobiographical sentences that begin with different alphabet letters. Challenge older students to create a sentence for each letter of the alphabet. Then have each child illustrate his pages and design a book cover for his book. To complete his book, a student sequences his pages alphabetically, then staples them between his book cover. Right down to the letter, these autobiographies are a great way for students to record their special memories.

Candy Whelan—Gr. 3, Garlough Elementary
West St. Paul, MN

A Happy Class!

Reinforce happy thoughts with a class "Happy Book." To make this class journal, cut out and staple a supply of circular writing paper between two construction-paper circles. Draw a happy face on the front cover. Program the first page with the title "Our Happy Book" and the current date; then place the journal and a special pen (perhaps one with happy faces on it) at a writing center or other desired location. Near the end of each school day, select a different student to write several sentences in the journal that describe a happy event from his day. Ask each child to sign and date his journal entry. Periodically write happy entries in the journal yourself. Then set aside time every week to read aloud the entries for everyone to enjoy. You'll find that these happy thoughts have a very positive effect on the ambience of your classroom! When the journal becomes filled with happy thoughts, make another one. If desired, make the completed journal available for overnight checkout.

Shirley Smith—Gr. 3, Lincoln Elementary, Huntington, IN

I get a kick out of...

Pam Crane

Staying In Step

Create a colorful foot character similar to the one shown to keep your youngsters in step with writing all year long!

- For a year-round display, mount the cutout and the title "Staying In Step With Writing" on a bulletin board. Have each student display a favorite piece of published writing on the board. Each month ask students to replace their displayed writing with more current samples.
- For a daily journal-writing prompt, tape the character to the chalkboard and draw a large speech bubble beside it. Each day program the speech bubble with a title, story starter, or other writing prompt. Students may choose to use the provided writing prompt for journal writing, or they may write about a self-selected topic.

The "Write" Foot!

Name _____

Use this pattern with
"The 'Write' Foot" on page 86.

Hooked On Journals

When we asked our subscribers to share their favorite journal activities, we quickly learned that teachers everywhere are hooked on journals! Whether you're just starting to use journals or you're a seasoned pro, take a look at the following teacher-tested tips and activities.

Special Entries

Sometimes children write journal entries that they especially want their teacher to read, but they are too shy to mention them. To solve this situation, ask students to fold down the top corners of these journal pages. At a glance you can see which entries are top priority.

Denise Evans—Gr. 2, Hodge Elementary, Denton, TX

Clip Art

Inspire creative journal writing with appealing clip art. Cut out a supply of interesting pictures from discarded magazines and newspapers. Duplicate student copies of each picture. Periodically distribute a set of pictures for a journal-writing exercise. Have each student glue his picture to a journal page and write a corresponding entry. Encourage students to write a variety of entries such as stories, poems, songs, letters, and personal anecdotes.

Vareane Gray Heese, Omaha, NE

The Literature Link

Combine journal writing, literature, and cooperative learning with this teaching suggestion. Divide students into cooperative groups and give each group member a writing journal, a list of literature-related writing topics, and a copy of the same trade book. During each group meeting, students reflect on their previous reading assignment and share their latest journal entries. Before the group dismisses, it determines the next day's reading assignment and selects a journal-writing topic. The group can choose a writing topic from the provided topic list or concur on an original one. This teaching strategy enhances students' comprehension and writing skills in a positive setting.

Cindy Ward—Gr. 3, Webster Elementary, Rushville, IL

All-About-Me Keepsakes

These yearlong writing journals become treasured keepsakes at the end of the school year. On the first day of school, present each youngster with a writing journal. On that day and every school day during the year, have students write journal entries that reveal something about themselves. For example, writing topics might include "The Funniest Day Of My Life," "The Five Best Things About My Family," and "Something I Really Dislike." Ask students to suggest additional writing topics.

Cindy Ward—Gr. 3

Thematic Writing

Here's a fun way to incorporate journal writing into your thematic units. Decorate a bulletin board with pictures related to your current unit of study. Behind or on the back of each picture, write a theme-related question, thought-provoking phrase, or story starter that can be used as a writing prompt. Each morning ask your daily helper to randomly choose a picture from the display and read its "hidden" journal assignment. For added writing motivation, provide youngsters with theme-shaped writing journals.

Andrea Johnson—Grs. K-3
Blanton Elementary
St. Petersburg, FL

Closing Sentences

Journal entries take on a whole new twist with this activity. Rather than providing a story starter or story title, provide the closing sentence for a story. For example, challenge students to write stories that end with sentences such as "That's what friends are for!," "They lived happily ever after," and "We all went home for cookies and milk." Students will delight in creating stories to fit the assigned endings.

Nancy Barondeau—Gr. 3
Edmunds Central Elementary
Hosmer, SD

It's My Turn!

Making sure that all youngsters have equal opportunities to share their journal writing is a cinch using this management system. Divide students into four groups. Color-code each group's journals by attaching the same color of adhesive dot to the journal covers. Next assign each group a journal-sharing day of either Monday, Tuesday, Wednesday, or Thursday. Reserve Friday sharing for students who were absent on their designated days.

Donna Gregory—Grs. 1 & 2

Journaling Center

This journal-writing center will receive rave reviews from your youngsters. Place your students' journals and a variety of pencils, pens, markers, and crayons at a center. Program the current month of a large wall calendar with daily writing topics; then display the calendar at the center. Students visit the center daily to write in their journals. Students may or may not use the writing suggestion for the day. They also have the option of working alone or with a friend. Write on!

Annette Rupert—Gr. 2
Colorado Christian School
Denver, CO

Creative Sharing

Using this plan, you can add variety and surprise to your journal-sharing routine. Label each of several cards with a different sharing option such as "Read to the class," "Read to a friend on your left," "Read to yourself," "Read to a small group," and "Put your journals away." Conclude each of your writing sessions by asking the class helper for the day to randomly choose and read aloud one of the cards. Then have students share their journals according to his instructions.

Maureen Pecoraro—Gr. 1   *Sally S. Hangliter—Gr. 2*
Cattaraugus Elementary   *Homer-Center School*
Cattaraugus, NY   *Homer City, PA*

A Traveling Journal

Build a bridge between home and school with a "traveling journal"—a journal that goes home with a different student each school night. Attach a parent letter to the front cover of the journal explaining that each child's assignment is to write and date an entry on the first available journal page. Be sure to mention that students choose their own writing topics. Also encourage parents to take time to read their children's journal entries and the entries written by other youngsters. This activity generates writing interest and increases parent/child interaction. Parents can plan on the traveling journal visiting their homes approximately once a month.

Donna Gregory—Grs. 1 & 2
Hodge Elementary, Denton, TX

Terrific Topics

Most students love to suggest journal-writing topics, so why not capitalize on this wonderful resource? Place a supply of paper slips and pencils at your writing center and encourage students to submit their ideas for journal-writing topics. Review each submission and place the approved topics in a container on your desk. Dispose of all others. Each day ask your class helper to draw a slip from the container and read aloud the day's journal-writing topic. You'll have a wealth of creative ideas and a beaming group of motivated writers.

Stephanie Chamblee—Gr. 3
Lomax Elementary, Deer Park, TX

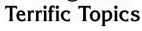

Journal Topics

Sticker Incentives

Your students will be stuck on journal writing with this super incentive program. On the inside cover of each child's journal, attach a 5" x 7" index card labeled "Story Stickers." Each time a child writes a predetermined number of sentences, attach a sticker to her card. When a student's card is filled, she takes it home as a reward for her writing accomplishments.

April Johnson—Gr. 1
Morningside Elementary
Perry, GA

Bunches Of Blue Books

College blue books (available in most college bookstores) make wonderful journals for young children. Because college blue books contain fewer pages than most spiral notebooks, students can fill the pages of their journals in less time. This creates an added sense of accomplishment for your youngsters and it allows parents to review their children's writing more frequently. And to top it all off, these nifty books are inexpensive to purchase!

Joanne Rosengren—Gr. 2
Nashotah, WI

Question Of The Day

If you're looking for thought-provoking questions to motivate your students' writing, this activity is for you. *The Kids' Book Of Questions* by Gregory Stock, Ph.D. (Workman Publishing, 1988), is filled with questions that children are eager to answer. Write one question on your chalkboard each day and have students respond to it in their journals. Your youngsters' journal entries will never be the same.

Adriana L. García—Gr. 2
Rowan Avenue Elementary

Timely Responses

Reading and responding to students' journal writing is an important factor to consider when implementing a journal-writing program. Here's a system to help you stay on top of this enormous task. Divide your students' journals into four or five groups. Using markers or colorful adhesive dots, color-code each group of journals. Then designate one day per week to read each group of journals. Students will be pleased with your timely responses.

Joanne Rosengren—Gr. 2

The Science Link

Here's a great way to integrate science and writing. In special science journals, have students record their science questions and hypotheses, science experiments, and newly acquired science information. Encourage students to share and discuss their journal entries with one another for increased comprehension.

Kelly McCalla
Oakland Elementary School
Greenwood, SC

Journal Walk

For a fun change of pace, try this unique approach to journal writing. Have each student open his journal to a blank page, then lay the journal on his desktop. Carrying only their pencils, students walk silently around the room and write messages, compliments, riddles, and questions in their classmates' journals. When the students return to their desks, they'll have an assortment of messages awaiting them.

Beth Ann Bill—Gr. 3
Lincoln Elementary
Merrill, WI

Welcome To A New Day!

Begin each day with a positive writing experience. Each morning while you are collecting lunch money, student homework, and/or parent notes, have students write in their personal journals. Periodically, attach a new list of topics to the inside cover of each journal for extra writing inspiration. As soon as you complete your tasks, begin to write in your personal journal, too. Each week set aside time for journal sharing. In addition, collect students' journals periodically and respond to their ideas and stories by writing brief comments beside selected entries. To reinforce correct spelling, try to include the words that a youngster is repeatedly misspelling in your written comments.

Deb Marciano Boehm—Gr. 2, Woodridge School, Cranston, RI

Fill In The Blanks

Here's a one-of-a-kind journal activity your youngsters are sure to enjoy. Ask each student to write a story on any topic he chooses. The catch to this story-writing activity is that each youngster must replace a predetermined number of key words in his story with blank lines. Then each student takes a turn reading his story aloud. When the student comes to a blank line, he asks a classmate for a word and inserts the word into his story. The resulting tales are truly one-of-a-kind creations!

Beth Ann Bill—Gr. 3

Questioning Journal Topics

For writing motivation, have students brainstorm questions about their writing topics. For example, if the topic is *food*, students might brainstorm questions such as *"Who* is your favorite lunch partner?", *"What* is your favorite breakfast food?", *"Where* is your favorite restaurant?", *"When* do you like to eat desserts?", and *"How* often do you eat meals away from home?" Students enjoy generating and responding to these questions.

Julie Minhinnett—Gr. 2
Westview Elementary
Richmond, IN

The Official Journal Prompter

It's official! Choosing writing topics for journal time is the responsibility of the daily journal prompter. You will need an official-looking cap and a decorated box. Place several strips of paper labeled with writing topics inside the box. Each day before journal-writing time, set the container of ideas at the front of the classroom. The official journal prompter for the day then dons the special cap and marches up to the box. He randomly chooses a slip from the container, then with authority, proclaims the writing topic for the day. Students love the presentation and eagerly await journal-writing time.

Joanne Yantz—Grs. 2 & 3 Language Resource
Woodfern School
Neshanic, NJ

What's Next?

Keep students actively involved in daily storytime sessions with this journal-writing idea. Each day conclude the story that you are reading aloud at an extremely exciting or suspenseful part. Then have students predict in their journals what they think will happen next. Encourage students to share their predictions with one another. Everyone will eagerly await the next storytime session.

Julie Vroon—Grs. 1 & 3
Rose Park Elementary
Holland, MI

Hooked On Writing!

Bait

This journal belongs to _____.

Date: _____ Grade: _____

Note To Teacher: Duplicate and use this journal cover as desired.

Just "Write" For Winter
Thought-Provoking Journal Ideas For December And January

Are you fearful that your youngsters' creative-thinking skills and writing expertise may stall out in wintertime weather? No need to worry. We've compiled a collection of weatherized writing topics that are perfect for any climate!

ideas contributed by Valerie Lathrop

How To Use Pages 97–100

To make journal writing extra special during the winter months, provide students with seasonally decorated journals. For December, duplicate student copies of the journal cover on page 98 on white construction paper. To make a journal for each child, staple a supply of paper between each journal cover and a 9" x 12" sheet of construction paper. Then have each child decorate and personalize his journal as desired. (For January, follow the same procedure using page 100.) For the best results, briefly discuss the writing topic of the day with your students before asking them to pen their thoughts and opinions. Write on!

December Journal Suggestions

The first day of December is World AIDS Day. If your best friend just found out that he or she had AIDS, what would you say to him or her?

December is Safe Toys And Gifts Month. What shopping tips would you give a Martian who is shopping for a safe earth toy? What toys would you suggest that he buy? What toys would you tell him not to buy?

Some of the most beautiful music in the world was written by famous German composer Ludwig van Beethoven, who was born on December 16, 1770. What kind of music do you like to listen to the most? How does this music make you feel? How would your life be different if there were no such thing as music?

On December 17, 1903, Orville and Wilbur Wright introduced a new form of transportation to the world—the powered airplane! What do you think will be the next transportation breakthrough? How will it be operated? What will make this form of transportation better than anything that we have now?

Joseph Grimaldi—known as the greatest clown in history—was born on December 18, 1778. Joseph began performing when he was only two years old and he clowned around for over 40 years! If you were a clown, how would you make your audience laugh? Would you enjoy being a clown? Why or why not?

Tell Someone They're Doing A Good Job Week is annually the first full week before Christmas. Why do you think it is important to let others know that they are doing a good job? What things do you think you do especially well? Do you think others notice your extra efforts? Why or why not?

The first day of winter is December 21. What do you think is the best thing about winter? What is one thing that could make this winter the best winter you've ever had? Why?

There are many homeless people in our country. On December 24, National Roof-Over-Your-Head Day, people are encouraged to help the homeless in their communities. How could you help the homeless in your community?

December is Bingo's Birthday Month. Why do you think people enjoy playing bingo? How would you change the game to make it even more fun?

What to do, what to do...

Make Up Your Mind Day is December 31. What do you do when you can't make up your mind? Is it more difficult to make up your mind about certain things? How would you help someone who is having trouble making up his or her mind?

This journal belongs to _____.

January Journal Suggestions
(See the instructions on page 97.)

The first seven days of January are Universal Letter-Writing Week. If you could ask one person in the whole world to write you a letter, who would you ask? Why would you ask this person? What do you think this person would write to you about?

Each January the top ten junk-food news stories from the past year are announced. Describe the best junk food you have ever eaten. What makes this junk food the best? How would you convince a friend to taste this junk food if he or she had never tasted it before?

"Weeks" Week is the first week in January. This week is to honor the other special weeks in the year such as National Week Of The Ocean and American Chocolate Week. If you could create a special week, what would you choose to honor? What would you suggest that people do during this special week?

Martin Luther King, Jr., was born on January 15, 1929. Dr. King wanted all people to live peacefully with one another. He worked hard to make his wish come true. If you could make one wish, what would it be? How would this wish improve the lives of all people? How would you try to make your wish come true?

January is Oatmeal Month. Oatmeal is a good-for-you food. What do you eat for breakfast? Do you think you eat healthful breakfasts? Defend your answer.

Pooh Day is January 18. A. A. Milne, who wrote *Winnie The Pooh* and *The House At Pooh Corner* (Puffin Books, 1992), was born on this day in 1882. What is your favorite story? Why do you think you like this story better than any others? If you were going to write a story especially for other children to read, what would you write about?

Hot And Spicy Food International Day is the third Saturday in January. Pretend that you have been asked to create a new hot and spicy food for the celebration. What will you make? How will you make it? What will happen when people eat your hot and spicy concoction?

National School Nurse Day is the fourth Wednesday in January. Describe the perfect school nurse. Do you think you would make a good school nurse? Why or why not?

The fourth Thursday in January is Clash Day. On that day, people wear colorful, mismatched clothes. Why do you think January is a good month for Clash Day? Do you think your school should celebrate Clash Day? Explain your answer.

National Puzzle Day is in January. What do you think is the best thing about puzzles? If you could design a brand-new kind of puzzle, what would it be? Why would people want to buy this new type of puzzle?

On Backwards Day, the last Friday in January, everything should be done backwards! What do you think would be the best part of Backwards Day? What would be the most difficult part? What would you do first and last on Backwards Day?

A WINTER WRITING WONDERLAND

This journal belongs to _____.

Note To Teacher: Use with pages 97 and 99.

Poetic Pursuit

The mystique and splendor of medieval days provide a perfect setting for your youngsters' early poetic attempts. This unit contains ideas for introducing several of the fundamental techniques commonly used in poetry. Since free verse encourages creative expression in a no-fail atmosphere, your young poetizers will be eager to give it a try.

by Karen Shelton

Treat Yourself Like Royalty

Inspire your students for any or all of these activities by having them create all kinds of medieval props (such as: castles, horses, dragons, armor, royal robes, scepters, thrones, flags, banners, crowns, and goblets) using the directions in *Once There Was A Knight And You Can Be One Too!* by Gregg Reyes and Judy Hindley (Random House Books For Young Readers, 1988).

Creative Castles

A day before this activity, ask students to bring in books containing illustrations of castles. (Another fun alternative would be to view a segment of Disney's *Robin Hood* or *The Sword In The Stone* video—having students watch with the intent of finding out about the castle in the story.) Display and discuss as many castle details as possible. Be certain to mention elements such as the gate, towers, thrones, windows, hallways, courtyards, stairs, and cellar. On the lower half of a construction-paper sheet, have each student use a black crayon to write one thing found in a castle. Encourage variety. After brainstorming several words to describe his noun, have each student write an adjective above it. Using the programmed papers, construct a bulletin board or hallway castle similar to the one shown. Have students read aloud their collaborative poem.

huge hallway		groaning door		colorful windows
	rocky walls		long table	
beautiful rugs		bright banner		damp cellar
	jeweled throne		dark dragon	

"Nonsenoetry"

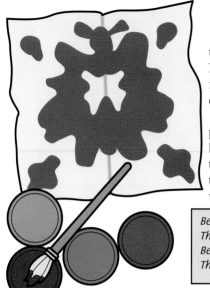

A lot of *nonsense* in a smattering of *poetry* equals *nonsenoetry*. Read aloud the book titled *Jabberwocky: From Through The Looking Glass*, illustrated by Graeme Base (Harry N. Abrams Inc., 1989). This medieval version of Lewis Carroll's classic nonsense poem is filled with portmanteau words—words resulting from the meshing of word pairs. (For example, *big* and *ugly* become *bugly*—which means big and ugly.)

Inspire your youngsters by having them create imitation inkblot pictures using folded art paper and tempera paint. When the papers are dry, have each student add facial features to his blob art. As a group, have students generate a list of *creatures* that the blob art reminds them of. Also make a similar list of words that *describe* the creatures. Encourage imaginative responses. Assist the students in pairing words from each list to make portmanteau words. Then have students write poetry using their nonsense words in the verse below.

> *Beware the [name of creature], my child!*
> *The jaws that bite, the claws that catch!*
> *Beware the [name of creature], and shun*
> *The [describing word] [name of creature]!*

Dynamic, Dastardly Dragons

Youngsters will love the drama in creating and describing dragons as they are introduced to alliteration. Have students work cooperatively to paint a long, long dragon on bulletin-board paper. (Or have students construct a cardboard dragon in which they can parade around. Complete directions can be found in *Once There Was A Knight...* by Gregg Reyes and Judy Hindley [Random House Books For Young Readers, 1988].) Then have students brainstorm a name for the dragon. Once a name has been selected, generate a list of descriptive words and synonyms for the dragon that begin with the same letter as his name. Have students choose their favorites and include them in a description followed by the dragon's name.

> *Different, dimply dingbat.*
> *Dark, delightful daredevil.*
> *He's Dudley, the dragon.*

Astride A Steed

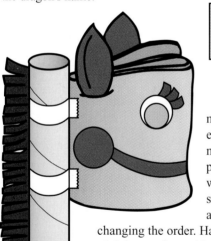

In medieval days, the trusty steed was essential to a knight's success. Determine how many of your students have ridden toy horses or carousel horses. Have them describe their experiences, employing as many sensory descriptions as possible. Then determine how many students have ridden real horses. Have them relate the experience to the class. If possible, show a film or video of a youngster riding a horse. Ask students to describe what it must have felt like to be a knight riding off to battle on a swift horse. Encourage students to include the sights, sounds, smells, and tactile experiences associated with such a ride. Record their descriptions on the board. If necessary, rewrite the descriptions, changing the order. Have students read and name their new poem. As a follow-up, have your students make stick horses from gift-wrap tubes, stuffed paper bags, construction paper, and craft scraps.

> *It feels a little dangerous.*
> *He smells like hay and dust and corn.*
> *As he gallops along, his mane whips my face.*
> *And his ears go forward and back.*
> *He's listening for "giddyap!"*

Jeweled Crowns

Youngsters will feel like royalty as they create crowns and conjure up a treasure chest of adjectives to describe them. In advance, spray-paint a variety of uncooked pastas several colors. Have each student dip pasta pieces in glue and place them on a tagboard crown cutout. Have students embellish their crowns with glitter pens and glue the crowns to construction-paper sheets. After the crowns are completely dry, write the word *pretty* on the board. Have students dictate synonyms for *pretty*. Discuss the resulting list and guide students in discovering the intensity of each of the synonyms. Then have students write *pretty* and its synonyms around the crown outline, and trim away the excess construction paper. As a follow-up to this activity, have each student decorate the back of a paper plate to simulate his facial features and hairstyle. Attach each likeness to a bulletin board beneath that student's crown.

102

Riddle Verse

After hearing a medieval story, give students a few verbal clues leading to the identity of the main episodes of the story, one at a time. Be certain never to reveal what's happening—just give clues. Episodes might include a duel, a swift horseback ride, a royal ball, a feast, or a dragon slaying. After solving each of your riddles, have each student (or pair of students) select an episode from the story to describe. Caution students to describe the setting without divulging the name of the event. Have students illustrate and display their poems.

> *Music and laughter fill the air.*
> *The soft swishing of long dresses is heard.*
> *The king and queen watch from their thrones.*

Onomato Who?

Young poetizers can have a great deal of fun with onomatopoeia. A portion of a video such as Disney's *Robin Hood* can be used as impetus for onomatopoeic verse. Preview the movie to find a segment that contains lots of action. Turn the television screen away from the class so that the students can't see the screen. Have students listen to the action. Rewind and replay the tape, listening for short periods at a time. Encourage students to isolate the main sounds they hear. Write the onomatopoeic words your students identify to describe the action. If a tape is unavailable, read the following sentences and have students make onomatopoeic substitutions.

Read to the students:	Possible Response:
The knight in heavy armor marches toward the dragon.	Clank, clank, clank.
He's so nervous his knees are knocking against the inside of the armor.	Tinkle, tinkle, tinkle.
The dragon heads toward him. Its giant feet slap the ground.	Boom! Boom! Boom!
The dishes in the townpeople's homes are jostled in the cupboards.	Clink, clink.
Suddenly, the dragon smiles and begins to sing a happy tune.	Fa-la-la-la-la!
The townspeople cheer wildly.	Yippeee! Yahooooooooooo!

Walk A Mile In His Armor

Youngsters put themselves in the places of medieval characters for this poetic writing activity. Have students describe what *fear* is and relate specific experiences in which they were afraid. Ask each student to imagine that he is a knight in battle with a fierce dragon. What are his fears? What is he thinking? As students dictate, write sentence fragments on the board. Later have each student write and illustrate a similar poem on his own.

> *Knees are shaking*
> *Heart is pounding, A lump in my throat,*
> *Too weak to do this.*
> *It's coming! Look out!*

Getting Published

As a culminating activity for your free-verse poetry unit, compile each student's favorite original poem into a book. Place this book in a reading corner for students to enjoy. Also provide copies of children's magazines with children's original poetry clearly marked.

In addition, consider submitting students' poetry to one of the magazines listed below for possible publication. These magazines receive a high volume of poems to choose from, so it's wise not to elevate your students' hopes of getting published. Submit copies of students' work, since the submissions will not be returned. (Send your students' poetry to only one magazine at a time. If a poem is selected for publication, ask the publisher before sending the poem to another magazine for consideration.)

- *Child Life,* P.O. Box 567, Indianapolis, IN 46206
- *Children's Playmate,* P.O. Box 567, Indianapolis, IN 46206
- *Jack and Jill,* P.O. Box 567, Indianapolis, IN 46206
- *Highlights For Children,* 803 Church Street, Honesdale, PA 18431

Bethanie H. Tucker
Alton, VA

Writing To The Rescue!

These teacher-tested journal-writing tips and activities are sure to save the day—without a lot of heroic effort!

1, 2, 3!

Increase students' journal-writing motivation with these three suggestions.

- The Buddy System: When writing time is over, have each student pair up with a buddy. Each youngster reads his journal entry to his buddy; then the buddies trade journals, and each student writes a positive response in his buddy's journal.
- Open Journals: Have students leave their journals open to their latest entries throughout the day. Journals can be placed on the students' desktops or at a writing center. During the day, students read their classmates' journal entries and jot positive notes to each other in their journals.
- Modeling: Keep a journal of your own and leave it on display for youngsters to read and respond to.

Janiel M. Wagstaff—Gr. 2, Bennion Elementary, Salt Lake City, UT

Topics, Topics, Topics

Add these motivational writing topics to your collection!

- Pretend that you are swimming and you find a treasure chest. Write a story about what is inside the chest.
- Pretend that you are a baseball. Write a story about being in a baseball game.
- Imagine that you and several friends live on a cloud. Write about your life.
- Pretend that you and your family have gone to the ocean. A friendly whale comes along and invites you to ride on its back. Write about your experience.
- Imagine that you have turned into a toy. Write a story about yourself.
- Pretend that you have become an animal for the day. Tell what kind of animal you are, and write a story about your day.
- Imagine that you are a newspaper reporter and you discover a footprint that is six feet long. Write a news story about your discovery.

Joanne Yantz—Grs. 2 & 3 Language Resource, Woodfern School, Neshanic, NJ

A Journal-Writing Corner

Corner your youngsters' creative endeavors at this writing center. Position a desk in a corner of your room. Atop the desk, place a timer and a small box. Inside the box, place a variety of items such as fabric scraps, small household utensils, and other unusual objects. A child brings her journal and pencil to the center. She sets the timer for five to ten minutes, chooses an object from the box to write about, and writes in her journal until the timer signals that her writing time is over. Change the contents of the box on a regular basis.

Heather Bradley-Mueller—Grs. K–2 Hearing Impaired
Montgomery County IU, Norristown, PA

Field-Trip Memories

Enhance the meaning of your class field trips by having students engage in this field-trip journal activity. Several days before your field trip, have each student make and decorate an eight-page journal. Then provide the following directions for completing the individual pages. (Pages 1 and 2 are completed before the field trip. Pages 3 through 8 are programmed before the trip and completed after the trip.)

Page 1: Write about the upcoming field trip. Include the following information: your name, your teacher's name, your school's name, the location, and the date of the field trip.

Page 2: Write about what you hope to learn during the trip.

Program pages 3 through 8 as follows:

Page 3: I saw...

Page 4: Here is a picture of one thing that I saw.

Page 5: I felt...

Page 6: Now I know that...

Page 7: My favorite part of the trip was...

Page 8: I would still like to know...

Encourage students to share their completed journals with their families and friends.

Sandy Bakke, Patton Elementary School, Austin, TX

Mathematical Explanations

Reinforce math concepts with journal writing. After introducing a new math concept, write a corresponding problem on the board. Then have each child write an entry in his journal that explains how to solve this problem. Describing the new math process in writing helps many children solidify their understanding of the concept. This is also an effective way to identify students who are experiencing difficulty in math.

Nancy Barondeau—Gr. 3, Edmunds Central Elementary, Hosmer, SD

Easy-To-Make Journals

These durable journals are easy to make and extremely versatile. To make each journal, staple approximately 20 sheets of story paper between two slightly larger wallpaper covers. (Inquire at your local wallpaper store for a book of discontinued wallpaper samples for this purpose.) Have each student use a permanent marker to personalize his journal cover. Give students the option of illustrating their written work when these journals are used.

Julie Malin—Gr. 1, St. Albert Primary, Council Bluffs, IA

Vacation Journals

To encourage students to continue their journal writing during school and/or family vacations, send youngsters home with special vacation journals. To make a vacation journal, staple a desired number of blank pages between two construction-paper covers. Have each student personalize and decorate the cover of his journal as desired. For best results also send home a parent letter explaining how the journal is to be used. A list of suggested writing topics could also be included. When the students return to school, set aside time for journal sharing.

Mary Ann Cacchillo—Gr. 1, Lafayette School, Shelton, CT

Getting The Scoop On Writing Reports

Keep your youngsters hot on the trail of report writing with these trustworthy ideas from our subscribers. Who knew that writing reports could be so much fun!

It's All In The Hand

Use this handy approach when teaching students to write simple reports or expository paragraphs. Show students your left palm with your fingers extended and give them the following writing tips. Tell students that first *(point to your left thumb)* a writer must introduce her topic. Next she states at least three facts about her topic *(point to fingers one, two, and three);* then she concludes her report *(point to pinkie finger)* with a summary sentence or a sentence that tells how she feels about the topic. Repeat the presentation, this time asking the students to join you in saying and dramatizing the tips. If desired also have each child cut out a duplicated hand shape that you've programmed with the writing tips and tape the cutout to the corner of her desk. Students will be eager to try out their handy writing tips right away!

Carol Ann Perks—Grs. K–5 Gifted, Comstock Elementary, Miami, FL

Four Facts

Report writing can be as easy as one, two, three, and four! Have each student fold a sheet of paper in half twice, then unfold the paper to reveal four boxes. In each box a student writes one interesting fact about her topic. Next she cuts the boxes apart and arranges the facts in a desired order. (This approach allows the student to rearrange the order of the facts an unlimited number of times.) Then, on a sheet of writing paper, she writes an introductory sentence about her topic, her four facts, and a summary sentence. There you have it—a four-fact report!

Debbie Fly—Gr. 3, Edgewood School, Homewood, AL

Boxed Reports

Any report topic and just about any clean, empty box will do for this creative report-writing project. To begin, a student covers his box with colorful background paper. Then, on white paper cut to fit each side of his box (and the top and bottom if desired), he writes and illustrates his report. For the best results, provide a few writing guidelines like the following: each box report must include a prominent title, the name of the reporter, five or more facts, and two or more illustrations. This creative approach to report writing is sure to bring unique and informative results.

Carol Ann Perks—Grs. K–5 Gifted

Waterfalls, little plants, interesting animals, and lots of rocks can be found inside caves.

People who explore caves are called cavers.

Only one person can get in small caves, but large caves can be more than 300 miles long.

Caves were often places of shelter along the Underground Railroad.

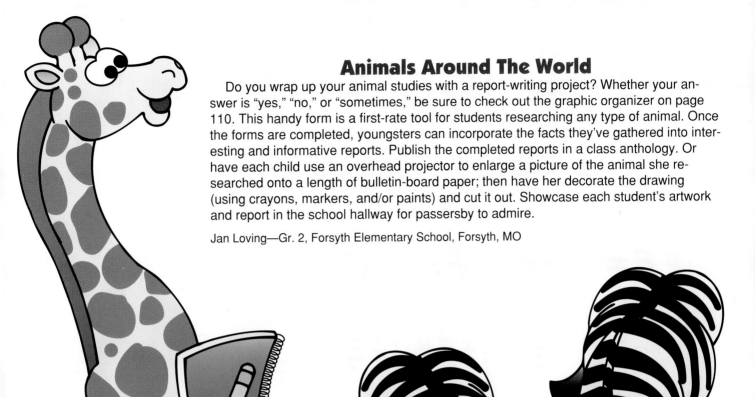

Animals Around The World

Do you wrap up your animal studies with a report-writing project? Whether your answer is "yes," "no," or "sometimes," be sure to check out the graphic organizer on page 110. This handy form is a first-rate tool for students researching any type of animal. Once the forms are completed, youngsters can incorporate the facts they've gathered into interesting and informative reports. Publish the completed reports in a class anthology. Or have each child use an overhead projector to enlarge a picture of the animal she researched onto a length of bulletin-board paper; then have her decorate the drawing (using crayons, markers, and/or paints) and cut it out. Showcase each student's artwork and report in the school hallway for passersby to admire.

Jan Loving—Gr. 2, Forsyth Elementary School, Forsyth, MO

It's In The Name

Just when students think you couldn't possibly come up with a new way to write a report—spring this idea on them! Have each student use a marker or crayon to write the assigned report topic in capital letters down the left-hand side of a sheet of paper. Each child then researches the topic and writes her report by creating a fact sentence for each listed letter. Younger students may wish to follow the pattern of "*C* is for…," "*L* is for…," and so on.

Or have each child use a crayon or marker to write the topic at the top of her paper, then write her first name (in capital letters) down the left-hand side. When taking this approach, assign a minimum number of facts that must be included in the report. This means that students with shorter names must include a letter or letters from their middle or last names, and students with longer first names may choose not to write a sentence for each letter in their first names. Your youngsters are sure to have loads of fun using this personalized approach to report writing!

Carol Ann Perks—Grs. K–5 Gifted, Comstock Elementary, Miami, FL

Rachel

T is for toadlet. It means a toad that isn't an adult.

O is for old skin. A toad sheds its old skin.

A is for amphibian. That is what a toad is.

D is for dark because toads can see in the dark.

The Three Rs

Nope! It's not what you think! These three Rs stand for "Researching," "Recycling," and "Reporting." For the research portion, a student chooses an animal to investigate. Then, without mentioning the name of the animal, he writes each of his four favorite facts about it on a separate 5" x 7" card. On a 9" x 12" sheet of construction paper, he illustrates and labels the animal. For the recycling portion, the student uses a large recycled grocery bag to create a backdrop for his project. To do this, he cuts away the back and the bottom of the bag; then he flattens the bag, keeping the blank side up. He glues one fact card in each corner of the backdrop. He also folds his animal illustration in half and glues it in the center of the backdrop as shown. Then he uses a crayon or marker to write "My Animal Report" and his name on the resulting flap. For the reporting portion, each child, in turn, presents his mystery animal to the class. First he reads aloud the four facts he wrote. Then he accepts an animal guess from three different classmates. If the animal is identified, he shows the class his illustration. If the animal is not identified, the reporter names the animal and then reveals his illustration. Whether you're wrapping up an animal unit, or looking for a unique report-writing opportunity, this project has plenty of kid appeal!

Barbara Cooper—Gr. 1, Tenth Street School, Oakmont, PA

Bugs In 3-D

Students will go buggy over these insect reports! To begin, each child researches an insect and writes each of four fascinating facts about it on a separate 5" x 7" index card. Next she creates an enlarged three-dimensional replica of the insect. The replica can be crafted in a variety of ways, including forming the bug from salt dough, then painting the dried project; fashioning the bug from modeling clay; or creating the bug from an assortment of arts-and-crafts supplies that might include construction-paper scraps, tissue paper, waxed paper, toilet-tissue tubes, pipe cleaners, and wiggle eyes. To assemble the report, a student mounts her insect on a cardboard or posterboard rectangle that she has labeled with her name and the name of the insect. Then she tapes a fact card to each edge of the rectangle as shown. Display the completed reports around the classroom. Your students will be so proud of their work that you may wish to invite other classes to tour your students' insect gallery. During each tour, have your student reporters stand near their projects so that they can answer any questions that visitors may have.

Rose Zavisca—Gr. 2, South Bend Hebrew Day School, Mishawaka, IN

Facts About The Famous

Researching famous people is lots of fun; however, sorting out all the interesting facts about a famous person can be overwhelming. The next time you assign a famous person report, program a copy of the graphic organizer on page 111 with one research question or guideline per quadrant; then duplicate a copy for each student. A student writes the name of the person he is reporting on in the circle; then, in each section, he takes notes that correspond to the programming you've provided. This information can then be transformed into a simple report or into a report that includes one paragraph for each quadrant of information gathered. Invite each star reporter to share his completed project with his classmates.

Connie Pinegar—Gr. 3, Mitchellville Elementary, Mitchellville, IA

Working From A Web

When your cub reporters are ready to advance from one-paragraph reports to multiparagraph ones, introduce them to a web. Have each child draw a large oval in the center of a blank sheet of paper, then draw four (or more) straight lines extending from it. Have students write a report topic in the oval, then engage them in brainstorming general ideas about this topic. For example, if the report topic is "the ant," general topics might include "body," "homes," "food," "jobs," and "interesting facts." List the students' ideas on the chalkboard; then have each child copy a different general topic from the list onto each line of his web. As each child completes his research, he notes facts about each general topic on his web as shown. When the note-taking is completed, show students how each general topic can be converted into a paragraph by rewriting each general topic as a main-idea sentence and each related fact as a supporting detail. Now there's a report-writing strategy that yields interesting reports *and* a better understanding of paragraphs!

Debbie Erickson—Grs. 2–3, Waterloo Elementary, Waterloo, WI

The Pocket Approach

When students know how to organize their research notes, writing reports becomes a lot more fun! To use the pocket approach, each child needs a tagboard or construction-paper folder. She writes her report topic on the front of the folder; then she opens the folder and glues up to eight library pockets inside, taking care not to glue any pockets over the fold line. Next the student slips a blank card inside each pocket and sequentially numbers each pocket and its card. Before she begins her research, she labels each pocket with a question about the report topic. Then, as she finds information pertaining to each question, she notes it on the corresponding card. When her research is complete, she converts each question into a main-idea sentence, and she uses her notes as supporting details. Take the pocket approach and writing reports becomes easy as pie!

Mary Boehm—Gr. 3, Webster School, Rushville, IL

Calling The Shots

After your youngsters have a few reports under their belts, try this approach to report writing. Begin by asking each child to choose his own report topic. Next have each student write his name and his report topic on an index card. Then, on each of five additional index cards, have him write a different question that he has about his chosen topic. Each youngster researches his topic and writes the answer to each question on the appropriate index card. If desired give each student a few extra index cards on which to record other fascinating facts that he discovers about his topic. When his research is complete, the student proofreads his cards and stacks them in sequential order, placing his personalized topic card on top of the stack. At this point the student chooses between using his index cards to give an oral report or publishing his report on the computer. Or he can do both! You'll quickly learn that the sky is the limit when students report on topics of personal interest!

Sr. Barbara Flynn—Grs. 2–3, St. Ambrose School, St. Louis, MO

Animal:

Physical Characteristics:

(Give details about what the animal looks like.)

(Draw and color a picture of your animal.)

Carnivore **Herbivore** **Omnivore**

(Circle one.)

by ____________________

Habitat:

Continent:

Food Chain:

Facts reported by ____________________

 Note To Teacher: Use with "Animals Around The World" on page 107.

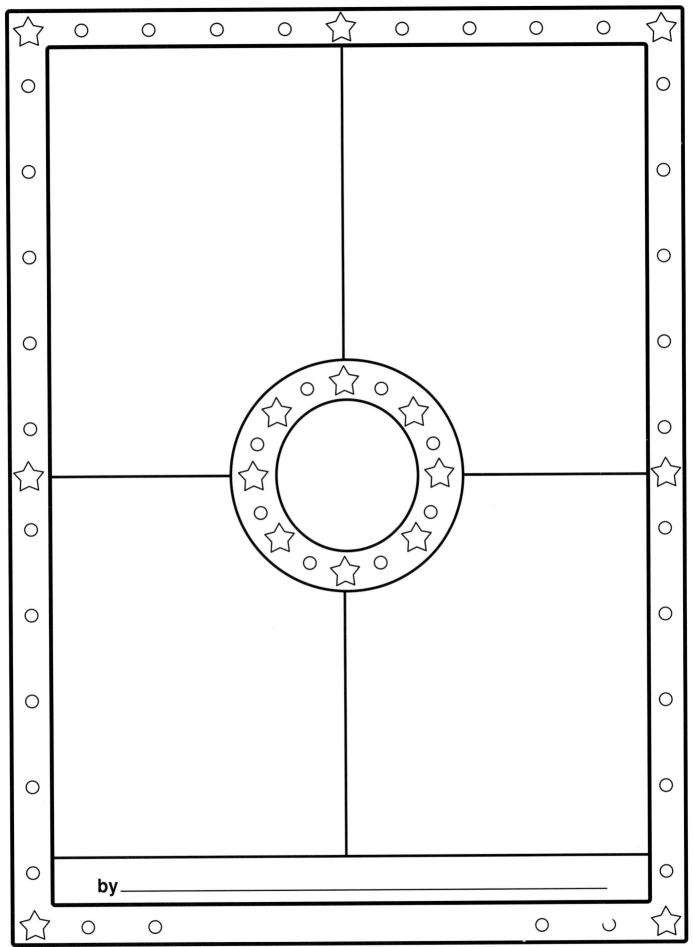

by _____

Sincerely Yours

Deliver year-round letter-writing practice with this collection of first-class activities.

ideas by Jennifer Overend

Special Delivery

Keep your youngsters' letter-writing skills in top form at this versatile center. On a length of decorated bulletin-board paper, write a friendly letter. Mount the letter; then label each letter part. Display an empty mailbox and an assortment of supplies such as writing paper, glue, scissors, and crayons. For your first letter-writing activity, duplicate student copies of page 114. Place the copies in the empty mailbox. A student removes an activity sheet from the mailbox and completes it. If desired, place a colorful envelope containing an answer key inside the mailbox. Once a student has completed the activity, he uses the answer key to check his work. After several days, deliver a new letter-writing challenge to the center.

Thanks For The Compliments

This activity builds positive attitudes, self-esteem, and letter-writing skills. Write your students' names on individual slips of paper. Place the names in a decorated container; then have each student choose one. Challenge each student to think of several reasons why she admires the classmate whose name she drew. Then have each student share her positive thoughts in a letter written to that classmate. Encourage students to mount their completed letters on construction paper and add a variety of decorations (using markers, tissue paper, glitter, and other arts-and-crafts materials) before presenting the letters to their classmates.

For a fun Valentine's Day project, have students mount their letters atop construction-paper hearts, then decorate the projects as desired. Students can deliver the resulting valentines during a Valentine's Day celebration.

Environmental Editorials

Challenge youngsters to express their environmental opinions by writing letters to the editor of a local newspaper. Have students brainstorm their concerns about several environmental issues such as acid rain, global warming, or solid waste. List these concerns on a large cutout that corresponds to the environmental issue. (For example, list acid rain concerns on a large raindrop cutout.) Next have each youngster choose one issue and in a letter to the editor, explain his concerns and suggest possible solutions.

Before mailing the completed letters, assure students that their letters will be read by the editor. Also explain that because editors receive large volumes of mail, their letters may not be published or answered. To guarantee that your youngsters' writing efforts are published, make a photocopy of each letter. Then publish the letters in a special environmental edition of your school or classroom newspaper.

Fairy-Tale Fan Mail

Writing letters to fairy-tale notables will undoubtedly thrill your young writers. For writing inspiration, read aloud *The Jolly Postman Or Other People's Letters* by Janet & Allen Ahlberg (Robert Bentley Inc., Pubs., 1987). In this delightful book, the Jolly Postman delivers unique correspondence to the fairy-tale characters along his route. Each piece of mail is stored in an envelope pocket and is a portable part of the text.

For a letter-writing activity, have each student write a letter inviting his favorite fairy-tale character to spend a day in his classroom. Before youngsters begin writing, determine a date for the visitations. Also inform youngsters that on this date they should plan to attend school dressed as the characters they are inviting. As the youngsters write their letters, make plans for the special guests. Could a fanfare of fairy tale–related activities be in order?

Dream Vacation

Before beginning this postcard project, read aloud *Stringbean's Trip To The Shining Sea* by Vera B. Williams (Scholastic Inc., 1990). In this delightful story, a series of postcards describes the adventures of Stringbean, his older brother, and his dog as they travel across the western United States. Once the story has been read, ask students to fantasize about their perfect dream vacations. Then have each youngster write a postcard to his classmates as if he were on this vacation. To make a postcard, have each student draw a line down the center of a 4 1/2" x 6" sheet of white construction paper. Then have each student write his message to the left of the line. To the right of the line, have each student copy the school address and design a colorful stamp. On the front of his postcard, have the student illustrate his dream vacation spot. After youngsters have shared their completed projects, suspend the cards from individual lengths of yarn; then attach the yarn lengths to a bulletin board titled "Our Dream Vacations."

Pam Crane

Dear Me!

Watch your youngsters' self-esteem soar as they pen these personal letters. As a prewriting activity, have each youngster complete a copy of the activity on page 115. Next, using his completed activity as a resource, have each student describe his positive traits in a letter written to himself. Once the letters have been written, have students decorate blank business-size envelopes, then fold and slide their letters inside. Encourage each youngster to keep his envelope in a special location so that he can easily retrieve and reread his letter. A good boost for self-esteem is never far away!

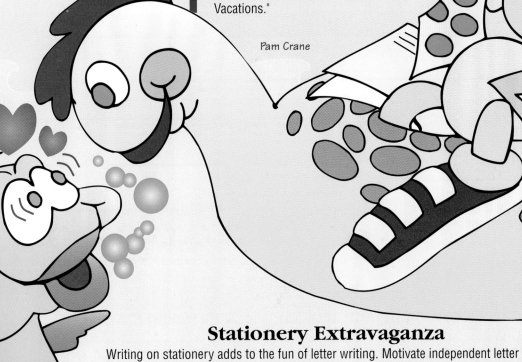

Stationery Extravaganza

Writing on stationery adds to the fun of letter writing. Motivate independent letter writing by providing a make-and-take stationery center. Or introduce the following ideas one at a time to younger students.

- Provide a variety of art supplies for students to use to decorate the borders of their letters. Supplies might include crayons, markers, glitter pens, rubber stamps, and stamp pads.
- Provide several large patterns and a supply of colorful paper. Students can create shape-stationery by tracing the patterns onto the paper, then cutting out and decorating the resulting shapes.
- Provide a supply of greeting cards. Invite students to glue their completed letters to the insides of the cards.
- Invite parents to donate leftover stationery pages and envelopes for letter-writing activities.

Airmail Delivery

Cut out the letter parts below.
Glue each part in place.

Bonus Box:

Use the color code.
Outline each letter part.

date—**blue**	greeting—**red**
body—**green**	closing—**purple**
signature—**orange**	

the woods. Today we made oatmeal cookies. Is Fido missing me? Please

I am having lots of fun at Grandmother's house. Yesterday we hiked in

remember to feed Wilbur every day. See you next week!

Your sister,   Polly

February 25, 1993   Dear Pete,

Note To Teacher: If desired, use with "Special Delivery" on page 112.

All About

_____

1. I feel happiest when _____

   _____

2. I think I am good at _____

   _____

3. I care about _____

   _____

4. Two words that describe me the best are _____

   and _____

5. I help out at home by _____

   _____

6. I know I am a good friend because _____

   _____

7. I feel best about myself when _____

   _____

8. I feel sad when _____

   _____

9. I am able to help out at school by _____

   _____

10. The thing I like best about me is _____

    _____

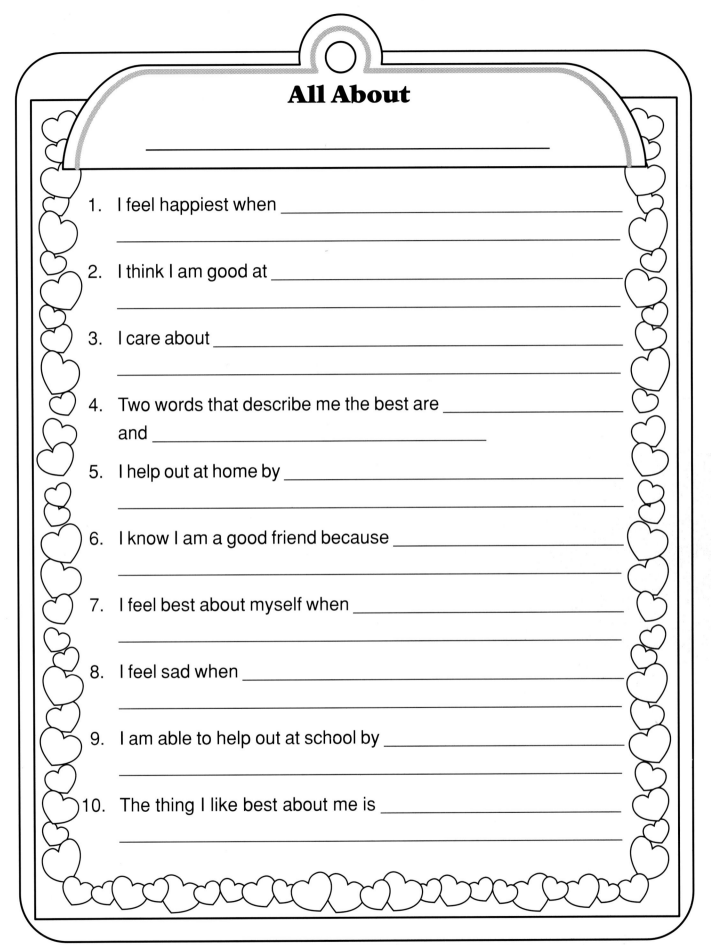

Note To Teacher: Have each student write his name on the line to complete the title; then have him complete the sentences. Use the completed activities with "Dear Me!" on page 113.

Name _____

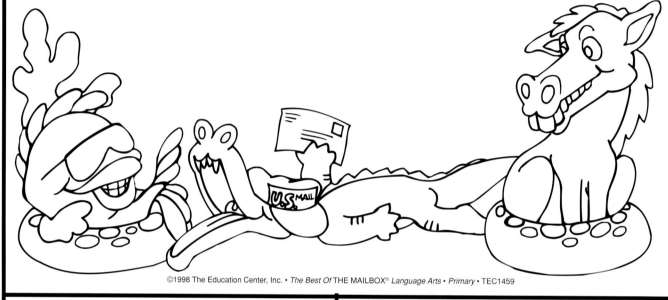

_____
(name)

earns a

Stamp Of Approval

for

_____
_____
_____

SPECIAL DELIVERY
SPECIAL DELIVERY

#1

Congratulations
on your
First-Class
Writing!

Note To Teacher: Use the open reproducible and duplicate and present the awards to students as desired.

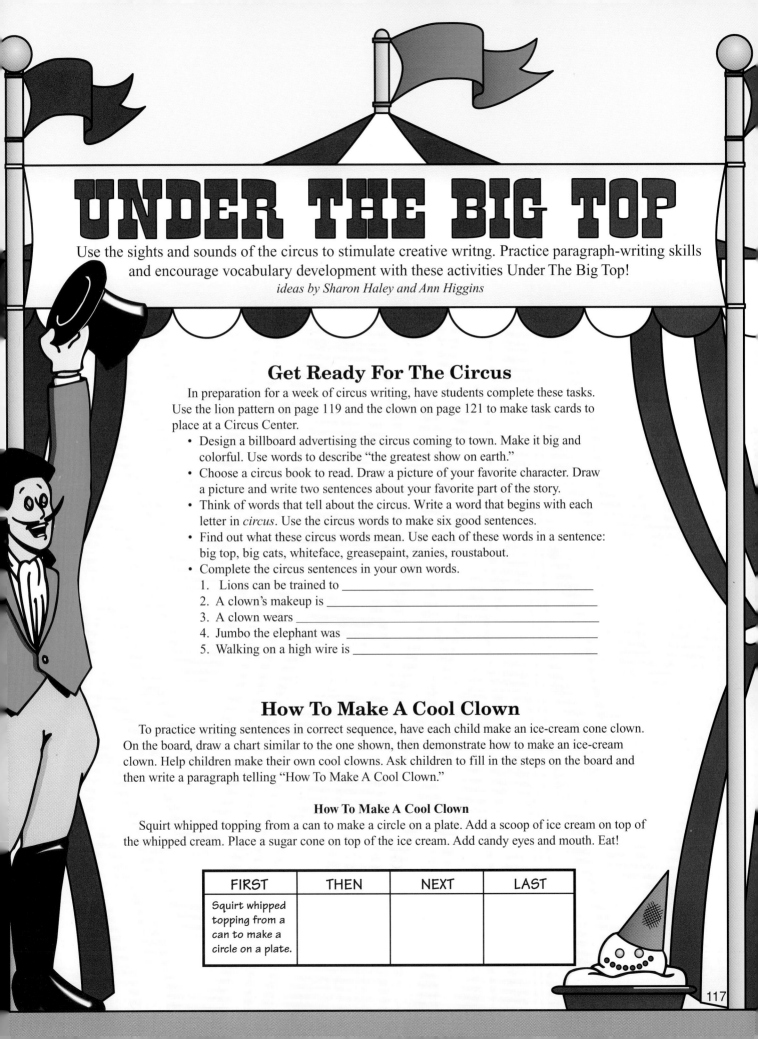

UNDER THE BIG TOP

Use the sights and sounds of the circus to stimulate creative writng. Practice paragraph-writing skills and encourage vocabulary development with these activities Under The Big Top!

ideas by Sharon Haley and Ann Higgins

Get Ready For The Circus

In preparation for a week of circus writing, have students complete these tasks. Use the lion pattern on page 119 and the clown on page 121 to make task cards to place at a Circus Center.

- Design a billboard advertising the circus coming to town. Make it big and colorful. Use words to describe "the greatest show on earth."
- Choose a circus book to read. Draw a picture of your favorite character. Draw a picture and write two sentences about your favorite part of the story.
- Think of words that tell about the circus. Write a word that begins with each letter in *circus*. Use the circus words to make six good sentences.
- Find out what these circus words mean. Use each of these words in a sentence: big top, big cats, whiteface, greasepaint, zanies, roustabout.
- Complete the circus sentences in your own words.
    1. Lions can be trained to _____
    2. A clown's makeup is _____
    3. A clown wears _____
    4. Jumbo the elephant was _____
    5. Walking on a high wire is _____

How To Make A Cool Clown

To practice writing sentences in correct sequence, have each child make an ice-cream cone clown. On the board, draw a chart similar to the one shown, then demonstrate how to make an ice-cream clown. Help children make their own cool clowns. Ask children to fill in the steps on the board and then write a paragraph telling "How To Make A Cool Clown."

How To Make A Cool Clown

Squirt whipped topping from a can to make a circle on a plate. Add a scoop of ice cream on top of the whipped cream. Place a sugar cone on top of the ice cream. Add candy eyes and mouth. Eat!

FIRST	THEN	NEXT	LAST
Squirt whipped topping from a can to make a circle on a plate.			

Big-Top Words

Begin your writing unit by reading several books about the circus to the class. Use the pattern on page 120 to make a large big-top tent on poster board. Laminate the tent and use a wipe-off marker to list circus words. Display the Big-Top Words for easy reference when writing begins.

THE BIG TOP

We See	We Smell	We Hear	We Taste
circus tent	popcorn	crowds	peanuts
clowns	hot dogs	roars	ice cream
acrobats	straw	ringmaster	cotton candy
horses	smoke	cannon	hot dogs
elephants	elephants	music	popcorn
show		toot	
magic		whistle	
trapeze		bang	
wild animals		boom	
lions and tigers		elephants	
parade			

Circus Sentence Pyramids

Have children work in committees to make sentence pyramids by adding more and more description to simple sentences. Demonstrate the pyramid idea on the board with this example:

I saw a clown.
I saw a funny clown.
My friend and I saw a funny clown.
My friend and I saw a funny clown at the circus.

Start with these sentences:
Look at the lion.   I see an acrobat.
I hear the band.   There is the tent.
There is the ringmaster.

Clown Faces

Having a big, red nose encourages descriptive paragraph writing! Have each student draw and color a clown face on a large sheet of construction paper. Give each child a balloon to blow up. Cut a small hole in each picture and insert a balloon nose. Ask each child to write a descriptive paragraph about his clown, giving as much detail as possible. Display the clown faces. In turn, children read their paragraphs aloud to see if the class can guess which clown is theirs. Display the paragraphs with the faces.

Clown Faces

Have students make circus booklets to review what they have learned about paragraph writing. Have the children write paragraphs to answer the following questions, one per page, and illustrate. Duplicate circus wagons on colored construction paper for covers. Have students personalize the circus wagon.

- What kind of circus performer would you like to be?
- What is the most exciting circus act? What makes it so exciting?
- What would you like about circus traveling?
- Which circus animal act do you like best and why?

Note To Teacher: Duplicate on tan construction paper to make task cards.

The Greatest Show On Earth

Cut and paste the sentences on the circus tent to make a paragraph.

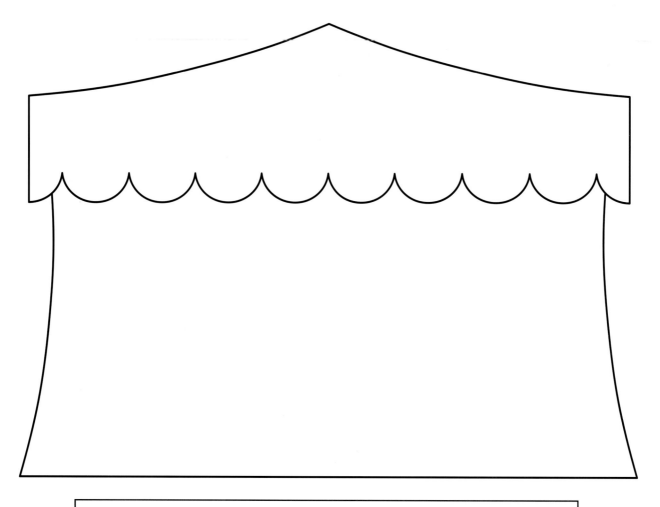

Bonus Box: Draw a picture to show what happened inside the big top.

Everything was ready.
Many people came to see the show.

Then the workers put three rings together.

The "Greatest Show on Earth" came to town.

First the workers put up the tent.

At last the clowns and animals marched around the ring.

Tubby The Clown

Color the topic sentence yellow.
Color sentences that go with the topic yellow.
Color sentences that do not belong red.

Tubby is the funniest clown in the circus.

I would like to be a clown someday.

Tubby's hair sticks out all over his head.

JoJo is the saddest clown.

Tubby throws pies at the other clowns.

One time he wore his shoes backward.

Bubbles is a clown, too.

Tubby is a funny guy!

Now read the yellow stripes to check your answers.

Bonus Box: Cut out Tubby's face and hat. Paste it on a long piece of paper. Draw the rest of Tubby!

My real name is _____ .

My clown name is _____ !

Funny Business

Read the chart below.
You can make up many different sentences.
This will help you write interesting paragraphs.

The	old		rode		funny	balloon.
A	skinny	clown	sat	on a	red	bike.
One	chubby		jumped		tiny	car.
That	sad		slid		polka-dotted	boat.

Now it's your turn to fill in a chart.
You get to do one about the lion tamer! Study the example.

The	brave		jumped		huge	leopard.
		lion tamer		at the		

Bonus Box: Use two of your sentences in a paragraph about the lion tamer!

Special Deliveries

From First-Class Pen Pals

Take a fresh look at the learning possibilities that pen pals offer. Whether students correspond across the country or down the hall, or send their messages by postal carriers versus electronically zapping them to their destinations, one thing is clear—the benefits of promoting pen-pal correspondence are enormous. So take a few minutes to read our subscribers' suggestions for ways to foster positive pen-pal relationships. It's a very special delivery that we feel certain you will enjoy!

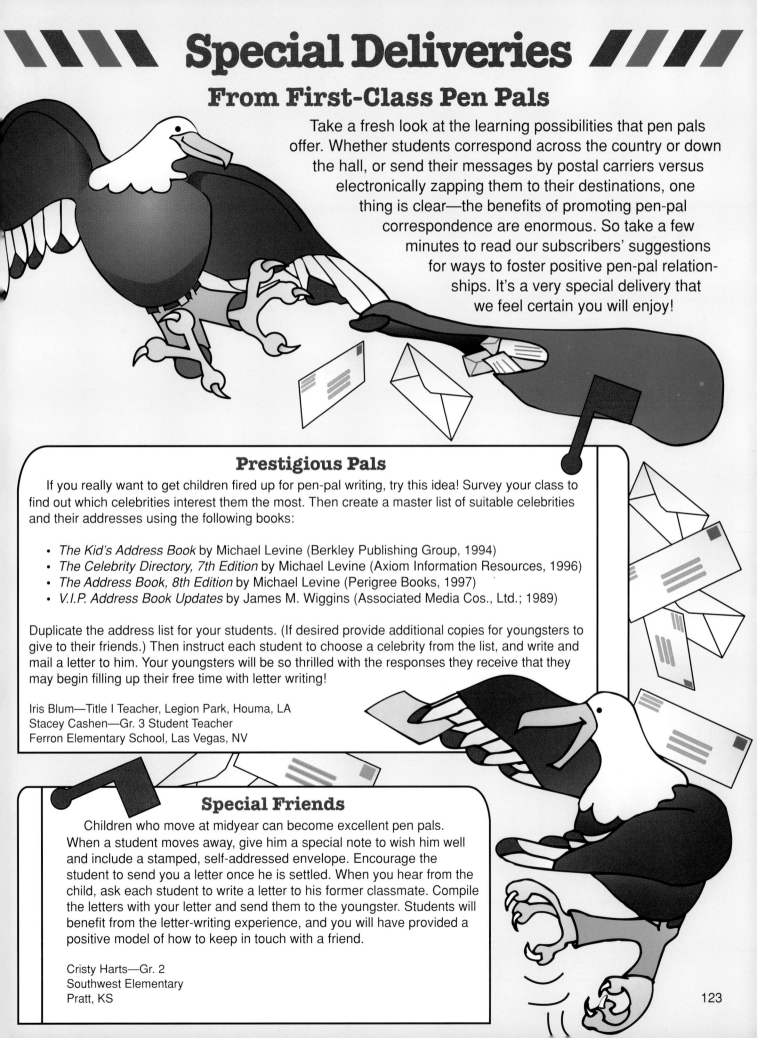

Prestigious Pals

If you really want to get children fired up for pen-pal writing, try this idea! Survey your class to find out which celebrities interest them the most. Then create a master list of suitable celebrities and their addresses using the following books:

- *The Kid's Address Book* by Michael Levine (Berkley Publishing Group, 1994)
- *The Celebrity Directory, 7th Edition* by Michael Levine (Axiom Information Resources, 1996)
- *The Address Book, 8th Edition* by Michael Levine (Perigree Books, 1997)
- *V.I.P. Address Book Updates* by James M. Wiggins (Associated Media Cos., Ltd.; 1989)

Duplicate the address list for your students. (If desired provide additional copies for youngsters to give to their friends.) Then instruct each student to choose a celebrity from the list, and write and mail a letter to him. Your youngsters will be so thrilled with the responses they receive that they may begin filling up their free time with letter writing!

Iris Blum—Title I Teacher, Legion Park, Houma, LA
Stacey Cashen—Gr. 3 Student Teacher
Ferron Elementary School, Las Vegas, NV

Special Friends

Children who move at midyear can become excellent pen pals. When a student moves away, give him a special note to wish him well and include a stamped, self-addressed envelope. Encourage the student to send you a letter once he is settled. When you hear from the child, ask each student to write a letter to his former classmate. Compile the letters with your letter and send them to the youngster. Students will benefit from the letter-writing experience, and you will have provided a positive model of how to keep in touch with a friend.

Cristy Harts—Gr. 2
Southwest Elementary
Pratt, KS

Pen Pals Down The Hall

For a fun and inexpensive writing experience, take these steps to develop an intraschool pen-pal program. Find another teacher in your school who wants pen pals for her students. Place a mailbox or another letter receptacle outside each classroom. Then pair each student with a child from the other class. After writing a letter and addressing an envelope to her pal, a student tucks the letter into the envelope and places it in the class mailbox. Each week assign a different youngster to be your classroom mail carrier. At a designated time each day, the mail carrier stamps each piece of mail with a rubber stamp before she delivers the correspondence to the mailbox of the other class. The mail's here!

Kellie S. Henry—Gr. 3
Kim Harper—Gr. 2
St. Joseph Grade School
St. Joseph, IL

From Batman® With Love

Spark an interest in writing when students pen these mysterious letters. Working with another teacher, pair your youngsters with students in an older class at your school. Keep the pairs a secret from students. Begin the letter writing by asking each older student to write a letter to an unnamed student-partner. Suggest that he include a few questions, so that the response will contain information about the recipient. For added fun have him sign his letter with an unusual pen name like Strawberry, Fred Flintstone®, Batman®, or Barney®. When each younger student has received and read his letter, have him write a letter to his secret pen pal, signing a fictitious pen name. After sending and receiving letters for a few months, combine the classes for a Pen-Pal Party. Youngsters will be all smiles when the secret identities are revealed!

Patsy Higdon—Gr. 3
Cynthia Neal—Gr. 5
Glen Arden Elementary
Arden, NC

Sister-City Pals

Here's a fun way to select a class with whom your students can correspond. Use an atlas to find a city with the same name as the town where your school is located. Send a letter to the city's Chamber of Commerce to find a school there. Then, at that school, contact a teacher of the same grade level to set up student correspondence. The newly paired pen pals will already have something in common: the name of their cities, *and* something to write about—what's happening in their towns.

Cheryl Escritt—Gr. 3, Gibbon Elementary, Gibbon, NE

Who's That Pen Pal?

Foster descriptive writing skills and stump your students' pen pals with this unique correspondence! Take a picture of each student. When the photos are developed, have each child refer to her snapshot to write a thorough description of herself. Also ask each child to label her letter and the back of her photo with an assigned number. Be sure to create a master list of the number assignments. Collect the photographs and the descriptions; then mail these items, along with the master list and a note, to the receiving class's teacher. In your note ask that the teacher mount the photos on a bulletin board and distribute the descriptions. Suggest that each child read and reread her pen pal's description until she can guess which photo shows her pal. Using the list you've enclosed, it will be easy for the teacher to verify the matches her students make.

Tina Marsh—Grs. K–5 Gifted Teacher
Jefferson Parkway Elementary
Newnan, GA

About Our School

Looking for a unique way to tell your pen pals about your school? Then this idea is for you! Tell your students that you will be working together to make a special booklet to send to their pen pals. First invite students to brainstorm sentences about their school as you write them on chart paper. Then have each child choose a sentence, copy it onto a sheet of white construction paper, and illustrate it. Collect the completed pages, compile them into a booklet, and drop the project in the mail. Your students' pen pals will proudly display this booklet in their classroom library and perhaps be inspired to reciprocate with a booklet about their school!

Suzanne Kulp—Gr. 2
Harrisburg Academy
Wormleysburg, PA

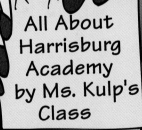

All About Harrisburg Academy by Ms. Kulp's Class

News Flash

We interrupt your regularly scheduled pen-pal correspondence to bring you the following videotaped news report. "Good morning, Pen Pals! This is Ryan Lee reporting to you from Silverthorne Elementary School's library. Let's step inside!" For sure, this isn't your typical pen-pal correspondence, but you can't beat it for creating interest between pen pals. Have each student select a school location (such as the playground, office, or computer lab) to be the focus of a news report. Encourage each student to write and rehearse an interesting report about the selected area; then videotape each student on location. Set aside time for your class to screen the completed project before mailing it to your pen pals. If you're lucky, your pen pals will include a news report in their upcoming correspondence, too!

Valerie A. Hudson—Title I Grs. 1–5
Silverthorne Elementary School
Breckenridge, CO

Great Connections

This puzzling project gives young letter recipients a lesson in teamwork. Have your students compose a special class message for their pen pals. Then use a marker to write the message on a large piece of poster board. Next have your students collaborate to create a decorative border around the message. Cut the poster board into pieces and give each student part of the resulting puzzle to include in a letter to his pen pal. Compile the students' letters and a note to the receiving class's teacher in a large envelope for mailing. After the recipients read their letters, they can connect their puzzle pieces to reveal the group message. What a great way to make connections across the miles!

Concetta Maranto—Gr. 3
Sandrini Elementary School
Bakersfield, CA

You Are The World's Best Pen Pals!

One of the nation's largest museums of carousel horses is in my town.

Hometown Homework

Give students something to write about by planning this homework assignment. Ask each child to research three facts about her hometown. After sharing her facts with the class, have each child incorporate them into a letter to her pen pal. Your students will think letter writing's a snap when they're armed with interesting things to write about.

Mary Dinneen—Gr. 2
Mountain View School
Bristol, CT

Treasures From Our Town To Yours

Pen pals will be delighted when they receive surprises from your town. Gather a number of artifacts that are native to your town or state (such as information from museums, photos of your town, postcards, and brochures of landmarks). If desired select a few students to write about the different items. Place the items in a box, along with the letters, and mail them to the pen pals. Your pen pals will treasure their surprises and will likely send some of their town's own artifacts in return.

Suzanne Buza—Gr. 2
Ben Franklin Elementary
San Antonio, TX

Map Of Our Town

Our Town

Dear Pen Pal

Worth A Thousand Words

When your students write to their pen pals, they'll probably mention classmates—and even you—from time to time. So that the people mentioned in the letters do not remain face-less, use this suggestion. Label a class picture with students' names and your name. Photocopy the labeled photo for each student's pen pal. The next time your students write to their pen pals, have them tuck these photos in the envelopes, too.

Carolyn Williams—Gr. 2
North Augusta Elementary
North Augusta, SC

First Row:
Second Row:
Third Row:

Mrs. Williams
Grade Two

Wow!!
He's one
tall dude!

Dear Curtis,
I am 78" tall.
Signed, Sylvester

Celebrity Responses

Engage your students in a graphing activity that has real star appeal. Have each student select a well-known person to write to. (Celebrity addresses can be obtained from the sources listed on page 123.) Ask your class to choose one question for stars to answer, such as "What is your height?" Have each child write the predetermined question on a stamped, self-addressed postcard. (If desired, each student can create his own postcard from cardboard that might otherwise be discarded, such as cereal boxes.) Then direct him to enclose it with a letter ex-plaining that the response will be used in a class assignment. When several cards have been returned to students, begin a class graph to chart the responses.

Ritsa Tassopoulos—Gr. 3
Oakdale Elementary
Cincinnati, OH

A Puzzling Idea!

Looking for a playful way to help your students' pen pals put names with faces? Then this idea is for you! Have a photograph of your class enlarged. Glue the enlargement onto poster board. On the back of the poster board, draw lines to create individual puzzle pieces. Then cut the pieces apart. Enclose the puzzle pieces and the original snapshot in an envelope, along with a letter that identifies each pictured person. Mail the project to your pen pals. The receiving class is sure to have a ball as they refer to the snapshot and piece together whom their new friends are.

Julie Plowman—Gr. 3
Adair-Casey Elementary
Adair, IA

More Special Deliveries!

In The Know

Encourage students to *really* get to know their pen pals with this ongoing activity! Have each child draw a Venn diagram on a sheet of drawing paper and label it with his name, his pen pal's name, and the phrase "How We Are Alike." Suggest that each student store his diagram in his desk for safekeeping. Then—as students learn about their pen pals' likes and dislikes, strengths and weaknesses, and families and friends—they record the information on their diagrams. The project is a fun way for students to learn about their new writing buddies, and it also encourages the students to include questions in their correspondence.

Concetta Maranto—Gr. 3, Sandrini Elementary School, Bakersfield, CA

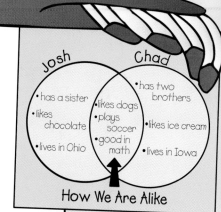

Front-Page News

Keep students informed about what's going on in their community and in their pen-pals' community with a front-page exchange. Periodically send the teacher of your students' pen-pals the front page from your local newspaper, and ask him or her to do the same for you. Each time a front page arrives, display it along with your local newspaper's front page for the same date. Then, as a group activity, compare and contrast the front-page news and the daily forecasts.

Tammy Brinkman and Kimberly Martin—Gr. 3
Dellview Elementary, San Antonio, TX

Special Deliveries

Simple enclosures can make your students' letters extra enticing to their pen pals. Some easy-to-mail treasures are newspaper clippings, stickers, riddles or jokes, illustrations, homemade puzzles, bookmarks, pressed flowers, and trading cards. Why not make plans today for every student in your class to tuck a special delivery into her next pen-pal correspondence?

Carole Curcio—Gr. 1
Hampton Elementary School, Hampton, NJ

A Pen-Pal Adventure

Strengthen the bonds between your students and their pen pals with a class-created pen-pal adventure. To begin, choose a story topic that can easily incorporate each pen pal as a character. Enlist your students' help in establishing the story's plot; then write a class-created story title and beginning on the chalkboard. Next have each student contribute a sentence for the story that features his pen pal. Record these sentences and a class-created story ending on the chalkboard. Edit the story as a class; then, on provided paper, have each child copy and illustrate the sentence that features his pen pal. While students are working, ask each one in turn to sign a page labeled "Authors and Illustrators." Also enlist

early finishers to copy and illustrate the beginning and ending of the story, and to design front and back book covers.

To assemble the book, enlist your students' help in sequencing the pages; then place the autographed page on top. Bind the pages between the student-created book covers; then carefully pack the project for shipping. You can count on this project receiving rave reviews!

Phoebe Sharp—Gr. 1 Special Education
Gillette School, Gillette, NJ

Math From Mail

After students read and enjoy a batch of pen-pal mail, use the corresponding postmarked envelope(s) to prompt this graphing activity. If your pen-pal letters arrive in a class envelope, create a class graph like the one shown. (If the letters arrive in individual envelopes, individual graphs will be in order.) Then, with your students' help, calculate and graph the number of days it took the correspondence to arrive. Repeat this activity each time a new batch of letters is delivered. Periodically find the average length of time it takes the letters to arrive, and challenge your students to estimate when the letters they send will be delivered to their pen pals. What an easy way to incorporate math into your pen-pal activities!

Concetta Maranto—Gr. 3
Sandrini Elementary School, Bakersfield, CA

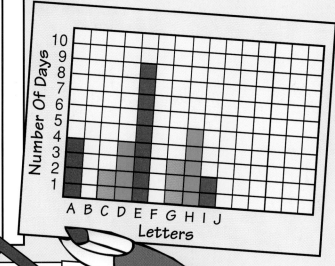

It's A Puzzle!

Your youngsters will have as much fun creating puzzle letters as their pen pals will have piecing them together! To make a one-page puzzle, a student writes his letter on a sheet of white construction paper; then he uses markers to decorate the margins of the completed letter. Next he turns the letter over, draws 10 to 12 large interlocking puzzle pieces, and cuts along the resulting lines. Have each student drop his puzzle pieces into an envelope he has addressed to his pen pal. Most likely the pen pals will reciprocate with similar letters, giving your youngsters the opportunity to piece together some correspondence, too!

Sandra Lee—Gr. 1, Wortham Elementary, Wortham, TX

Pictorial Postcard

Add pizzazz to pen-pal correspondence with student-designed postcards. Have each student draw a different scene or landmark from your local community on one side of a blank 5" x 7" card. On the other side, have each child write a note about the landmark, leaving room for a stamp and an address. Mail each card individually at the standard postcard rate, or package them together to send to your pen-pal class. Your students will not only be practicing their writing skills; they'll be learning about local points of interest and refining their artistic talents, too!

Deborah Ross—Gr. 3
Glen Arden Elementary School, Arden, NC

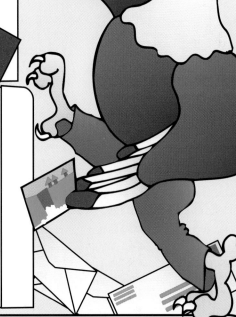

Just The Facts...From A To Z

Here's a letter-writing challenge that's sure to earn your students' stamp of approval! Have each child use crayons or colored pencils to list capital letters from *A* to *Z* down the left-hand side of a sheet of lined paper. Next have each child write a topic she would like to describe at the top of the paper. Topics might include herself, her family, her school, or her community. Then—following the pattern of "A is for…," "B is for…," and so on—she creates a sentence about her chosen topic for each alphabet letter. Have each student tuck her project and a brief letter of explanation in an envelope to her pen pal. The receiving pen pal is sure to get the facts from *A* to *Z* and may even feel compelled to share an alphabetized set of facts in return!

Carol Ann Perks—Grs. 1–5 Gifted
Comstock Elementary, Miami, FL

Straight From The Hive

"Bee-Dazzling" Ideas For Classroom Publishing

Do you find yourself wishing you had some fresh ideas for writing motivation, bookmaking projects, and publishing your youngsters' literary accomplishments? Well, thanks to our "bee-loved" subscribers, this honey of a unit is swarming with suggestions!

Monthly Newsletter

Have you ever considered publishing youngsters' literary efforts in a monthly parent newsletter? In addition to listing students' birthdays, units of study, upcoming events, and suggestions for skill reinforcement, feature several student-authored selections. Students are thrilled to find their pieces in the newsletter and are continually motivated to write quality stories, poems, and reports for possible publication.

Nancy Wojcik—Gr. 2
Hayes Elementary School
Kennesaw, GA

Big-Book Picture Show

Publishing big books is a major writing accomplishment for youngsters. Rather than simply shelving the books when the writing project is completed, consider republishing the books in the following manner: Photograph the front cover and each page of a child's big book; then have the resulting negatives made into slides. Using a slide projector, a screen, and optional background music, each author narrates a slide presentation of his big-book project. Students are certain to enjoy sharing their work through this unique media. Gee, why not take this show on the road?

Andrea Johnson—Grs. 1 & 2
Rawlings Elementary
Pinellas Park, FL

Classroom Collectables

Sweeten youngsters' enthusiasm for classroom publishing by displaying their work in an exclusive corner of the classroom. Arrange a bookcase and/or coffee table, a sofa, padded chairs, or pillows in the chosen corner. Display students' books in the area, taking care to spotlight the most recent publications. Books published by your previous classes could also be made available for perusing.

Leslie Simpson
San Diego, CA

Rave Reviews

Strengthen the home-school connection and boost your youngsters' writing confidence using this one-of-a-kind plan. In a parent letter, explain that each child will be bringing home his most recently published book. Ask that the parents read the books, write positive reviews about the books, and return the books and reviews to school by a designated date. When all of the reviews are in have each child read the review that was written about his book. Outstanding!

Kim Byrd—Gr. 3
Deer Run Elementary
Dublin, OH

Pam Crane

The Weekly News

Here's a publishing idea that's certain to receive rave reviews. On a sheet of poster board, create a newspaper form like the one shown below. Laminate the form. You will also need a supply of wipe-off markers in a variety of colors. To introduce the project, ask students to recall important or interesting events from the past school week. List these events on the chalkboard; then, with your youngsters' input, write the weekly headline and article, and complete the remaining features. Ask one student volunteer to illustrate the weekly headline and another to create a cartoon strip in the spaces provided. Post the completed project outside your classroom door. A week later, wipe away the programming and repeat the activity. If desired, group older students in newspaper staffs and have the staffs create the weekly newspapers on a rotating basis.

Dianne Neumann—Gr. 2
Frank C. Whiteley School
Hoffman Estates, IL

Roepke's Publishing Company

Wow! A genuine publishing company! Each week ask students to submit a writing sample to your publishing company. Place the youngsters' work in personalized file folders. At the end of six weeks, remove each student's work from his file folder and bind it between construction-paper covers. Have students illustrate and personalize the covers of their "published" books. After students have shared their latest literary releases with their families and friends, display them in your classroom library.

Kim Roepke
Tullahomer, TN

Student Anthologies

This grown-up approach to publishing keeps youngsters as busy as bees. Discuss the meaning of *anthology* with students; then have each student label a colorful folder "[student name]'s Anthology." When the folders are decorated, store them in a central location. Throughout the year have students select literary pieces to place in their personalized folders. By the year's end, each student has an outstanding anthology to his credit.

Penny Blazer—Gr. 1
Penns Valley Elementary
Spring Mills, PA

Writing To Go

These classroom publications won't be gathering dust! Purchase a supply of three-ring binders. Each time your youngsters complete a writing project, compile their work in a binder. Ask a student volunteer to create and insert a corresponding title page. Using an established checkout system, students may take these published works home to share with their families and friends.

Barb Sandberg—Gr. 2
Christ The King School
Browerville, MN

Schoolwide Sharing

Published authors deserve to be recognized! To promote your young writers, make arrangements for them to visit other classrooms to share their written compositions. Or invite neighboring classrooms to your room for informal author readings. Students who prefer to avoid the limelight may choose to loan their books to neighboring classrooms or to the school library for independent reading.

Diane Afferton—Gr. 3
Chapin School
Morrisville, PA

Neumann News

Tadpoles Hatched!

Math Marvels

Really Fun Reading!

Artist Discovered!

Book Review

Comics

By Invitation Only

Add a touch of elegance to book-sharing events by inviting a special guest to each reading celebration. Guests might include your school principal, the police chief, a local author, or a radio or television celebrity in your area. Your students and their guests will feel honored to be a part of these unique celebrations.

Barb Sandberg—Gr. 2

Cub Reporters

Publishing a monthly student-written newsletter provides terrific writing motivation for your cub reporters. Each month have students submit articles for publication. These articles can be written about specific classroom events, special guests, assemblies, field trips, and children who celebrated birthdays during the month. Also encourage students to submit poetry and artwork for publication. Set a deadline for submissions; then, after making your final selections, ask a parent volunteer to type and format the newsletter on a school computer. (Ask your media or computer specialist to help you find an appropriate computer program for this purpose.) Students will beam with pride when they see the completed projects. Extra! Extra! Read all about it!

Helen F. Toy—Gr. 1
Balboa Boulevard Magnet School
Northridge, CA

Impressive Presentations

Over time do your students appear to lose interest in publishing their written endeavors? To keep students interested, plan monthly author-sharing events. In October plan a Spookfest. Arrange several pumpkins and a large bale of hay in front of a student-painted backdrop. Then, in turn, invite student authors to share their published works. Other monthly events could include an Applefest, a Turkeyfest, and a Snowfest. Fun!

Donna Tobey—Gr. 1
Gulliver Academy
Coral Gables, FL

WRITE ON!

Bulletin-Board Publishing

Remember—classroom publishing is not restricted to bookmaking! Displaying student stories on an attractively decorated bulletin board is also an effective and rewarding form of publishing. For ease, designate a board like the one shown above for year-round publishing.

Leslie Simpson
San Diego, CA

Authors' Tea

Reward published authors with a special tea in their honor. If desired, ask each student to meet a publishing goal such as ten books. Once several authors have met the goal, plan an Authors' Tea. Allow each featured author to invite a predetermined number of guests to the gathering. Enlist the rest of the youngsters in planning and preparing refreshments and decorations for the special event. At the tea, after the featured authors have each shared a favorite publication, serve refreshments. Plan additional teas as more authors meet the agreed-upon publishing goal. Write on!

Denise Quinn—Gr. 1
Mill Lake School
Spotswood, NJ

Big Book Of Favorites

This publishing project is a team effort. To begin, write each youngster's name on a slip of paper and deposit the papers in a basket. Next create a big book of blank pages. (Bind the book with plastic or metal rings so additional pages can be added.) At the conclusion of each read-aloud, draw a student's name from the basket. Ask that student to illustrate and write a sentence about his favorite part of the story on a blank booklet page. Keep this ongoing booklet project on display throughout the year. Students and classroom visitors will enjoy perusing this impressive publication.

Chris Irick
St. Rose School
Great Bend, KS

Books For Buddies

Inspire your youngsters to write by asking them to create books for their underclass buddies. Ask a colleague who teaches at a lower grade level what upcoming themes she has planned. Then have your youngsters write and publish books related to one of these themes. Once students have practiced presenting their books, make arrangements for them to share their creative endeavors with the youngsters for whom these books were written. Your authors and their audience will feel very special!

Pam Williams—Gr. 3
Dixieland Elementary School
Lakeland, FL

Appealing Publications

This publishing tip will save you hours of frustration! For those special occasions when you plan to type the text for your students' picture-book publications, a box of self-adhesive labels is a necessity. Type each sentence on a label. Students can attach the labels to their illustrations as desired. Trying to determine where to position the type on the individual pages is over. Try it! You'll love it!

Tammy Schuman
Copper Canyon School
Scottsdale, AZ

Cut here.

All About The Authors

When an individual writes a book, completing an author page is a fairly simple task. But what do you do when the entire class participates in a publication? Here's the answer! Attach a photocopy of your class picture to a blank page at the back of the book or to the book's back cover. Then have each youngster write a one-line autobiography to accompany the picture. Easy and effective!

Laura Rosen Horowitz—Gr. 2
Embassy Creek Elementary
Cooper City, FL

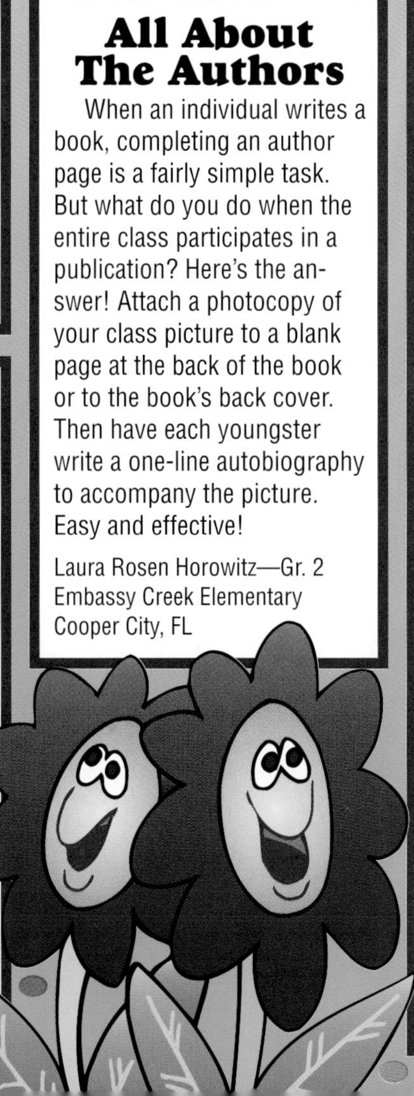

Paper-Bag Booklets

Students' writing is in the bag with this unique publishing project! Ask each youngster to bring three or more plain, brown paper lunch bags from home, or supply the bags yourself. To make a booklet, cut away the bottom of each paper bag. (See the illustration above.) Hole-punch two holes near the cut edge of one bag. Then, using this bag as a guide, punch two holes in the remaining bags. Stack the bags and align the holes. Thread a length of twine through each set of holes and securely tie the ends. Students find writing and illustrating stories in these unique booklets to be lots of fun! If desired, have each student write and illustrate an adventure that features a classmate as the main story character.

Jeannette Freeman—Gr. 3
Baldwin School of Puerto Rico
Guaynabo, Puerto Rico

Reading Recitals

Showcase your youngsters' writing talents at reading recitals. Plan the hour-long evening events several times throughout the school year. At each recital spotlight selected student authors. To prepare for a recital, a participating author creates an eye-catching display of his published works, practices reading aloud his favorite story or poem, and invites his family and friends to the event. If possible, videotape each recital so that the participating authors and their classmates can view it the following day. Bravo!

Betty Kobes—Gr. 1
Kanawha Elementary School
Kanawha, IA

Fantasy Stories

To set the stage for writing fantasy stories, ask each student to bring to school the front panel of a cereal box that features a make-believe character. Then have each youngster write and illustrate a story about himself and the fantasy character. Bind the completed stories between the cereal-box panels (front covers) and poster-board back covers of equal size. When the projects are completed, plan a before-school breakfast. After the meal, invite students to share their cereal-box adventures.

Donna Tobey—Gr. 1
Gulliver Academy
Coral Gables, FL

Booklets Galore!

Just the sight of dozens of uniquely made blank booklets can provide tons of writing motivation. With the help of volunteers, keep a supply of blank booklets on hand at all times. Books of different sizes and shapes are most appealing. Covers made from colorful construction paper, poster board, and wallpaper, and bound with different types of rings and yarn add to the books' charm. When a student is ready to publish a piece of writing, he simply chooses a book and copies and illustrates his edited version of the story inside.

Juliann S. Thrush—Gr. 1
Dream Lake Elementary School
Apopka, FL

Involving Parents

Classroom publishing can create huge demands on a teacher's time. Involving parents in the publication process helps you meet the writing needs of your students. Throughout the school year, recruit and train adult volunteers to assist you with a variety of publishing needs such as gathering materials, making booklets, and conferencing with individual writers. Parents could even be asked to maintain and run a bookmaking center in your classroom. Everyone benefits when you share the load.

Linda Benedict—Gr. 2, Indian Lake Elementary, Huntsville, OH
Dorothea Uniacke—Gr. 1, Fisher School, Walpole, MA

Schoolwide Publishing Center

Rather than having a "publishing company" in each of several classrooms in your school, why not join forces with your teaching colleagues and open a schoolwide publishing center? In the center, store desired cover-making supplies, including a laminator and a bookbinding machine. Ask parent volunteers to assist you in setting up and maintaining the center. When a student has written and illustrated the pages of his book, he visits the publishing center. Here an adult volunteer assists him in making a cover. If desired, title pages, dedication pages, and author pages could also be completed at the publishing center.

Michele Lasky—Gr. 1
Mandalay Elementary School
Wantagh, NY

Writing Extravaganza

Turn your youngsters on to writing with a bit of glitz and glitter! Equip a writing center with a variety of colorful pens and pencils. Also provide materials for making and decorating unique booklet pages. For example, provide several large patterns and a supply of colorful writing and construction paper. Students can create shape booklets by tracing the patterns onto the paper, then cutting out, decorating, and stapling together the resulting shapes. Crayons, markers, glitter pens, rubber stamps, and stamp pads can be used to decorate the booklet pages.

Michele Lasky—Gr. 1

Wordless Publications

For a creative alternative to the writing process, consider having your youngsters publish wordless books. Begin by "reading" and discussing a wordless picture book like Nancy Tafuri's *Junglewalk* (Greenwillow Books, 1988). Then have each student brainstorm a series of pictures that tell a story. Ask each student to draw a rough sketch of each picture he plans to include in his wordless book. Next pair students and have them discuss their projects and make any desired revisions. Then, working individually, have each student complete the final drawings for his book. Bind the completed illustrations between construction-paper covers. Give each youngster the opportunity to share his completed project with his classmates.

Diane Fortunato—Gr. 2
Carteret School
Bloomfield, NJ

Author Celebrations

Periodically commemorate the literary accomplishments of your student authors with surprise author celebrations. Serve simple refreshments and ask each youngster to read aloud his latest publication. This bit of recognition goes a long way toward keeping your student authors motivated.

Nancy Dunaway
Hughes Elementary School
Hughes, AR

Book-Assembling Party

Keeping a publishing center equipped with plenty of ready-to-use booklets is a time-consuming task. Although parent volunteers are usually willing to help out in this area, the job can become mundane. For a change of pace, invite the parents to your home on a Saturday afternoon for a book-making party. In addition to making loads of books for your publishing center, you'll have a wonderful time becoming better acquainted with your volunteers.

Nancy Dunaway

Publicizing Publications

Follow up your students' next publishing project with a media campaign. After displaying their completed books in the school library, have your young authors design eye-catching posters advertising their latest publications. Make arrangements for students to display their completed posters throughout the school. Your authors' readership is sure to increase!

Nancy Dunaway

Springtime Tea

As the school year comes to a close, take time to applaud the accomplishments of your student authors at an Authors' Tea. Announce the upcoming event in a parent letter; then make arrangements for parent volunteers to provide appropriate refreshments. During the tea, each student shares her favorite published work from the school year. This event will definitely receive two thumbs-up from the audience and the participants!

Carol C. Greenlund—Gr. 3
Camp Hill, PA

Familiar Faces

Your youngsters' book illustrations can take on a whole new look with this clever idea. Photocopy a supply of your students' most current school photographs. Cut apart and store the reproductions in personalized envelopes at a center. If a student wishes to feature himself or one of his classmates in an illustration and does not wish to render the facial portion of the picture himself, he simply cuts out and attaches a photocopied reproduction of the person's school picture. The illustrations often prove to be quite interesting!

Denise N. Morgan—Gr. 2
Kildeer Countryside School
Northbrook, IL

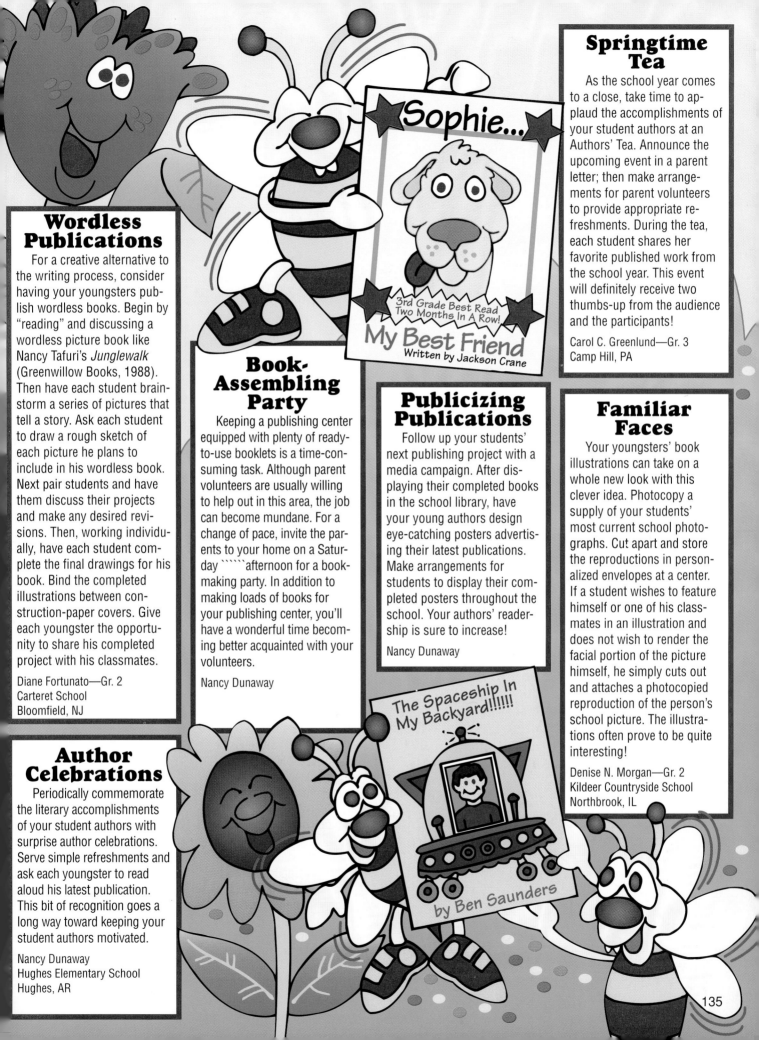

Sophie...

3rd Grade Best Read Two Months In A Row!

My Best Friend
Written by Jackson Crane

The Spaceship In My Backyard!!!!!

by Ben Saunders

About The Author

Spotlight student authors with easy-to-complete author pages. Duplicate a supply of author pages like the one shown. Also photocopy a supply of each child's school picture. A student glues a copy of his school picture in the box and completes the page using current information. Then he includes the page at the back of his published book. Students feel like "real" authors and enjoy the recognition they receive as a result of these personalized pages.

Denise N. Morgan—Gr. 2
Kildeer Countryside School
Northbrook, IL

All About The Author

Name __Karl Santos__
Age __8__
Hobbies __soccer,__ __rock collecting__
Other published books __The Peanut-Butter Alien__ __Undersea Treasure__

Poetry On A Badge

If your school has a badge maker, take advantage of this unique poetry-publishing idea. Following the directions provided with your badge maker, help each student publish an original poem on a badge. These publications will be worn with pride!

Pamela Schmieder—Gr. 2
Wilson Elementary
Zanesville, OH

Our Favorite Pieces

With this method of publishing, students can easily share their favorite literary pieces. All you need is a three-ring binder containing a plastic sleeve for each student. When a student wishes to "publish" a story or other written work, he simply slips it inside a plastic sleeve in the classroom binder. Later, when he is ready to publish a different selection, he replaces the previously published piece with a more current writing sample. If desired, students may also publish accompanying illustrations. This classroom collection is sure to be well read by students and classroom visitors.

Stacy Barrett Stuttard
Allegheny 1
Altoona, PA

Night

Night is like a bat flying in the sky.
Night is like the stars falling on me.
I love Night.
The Night falling on me.
—Stacie Welch
1993

Year-Round Binder

Durable, economical, and versatile accurately describe this year-round publishing strategy. All you need is a large three-ring binder, a supply of top-loading 9" x 12" plastic protectors, and several tabbed divider pages (optional). Decorate the cover of the binder as desired. To "publish" a literary work, a student obtains a plastic sleeve from you, slips his writing inside, and places it in the binder. If desired, label tabbed dividers with literary categories such as "Poetry," "Mysteries," and "Autobiographies," and ask students to publish their compositions in the appropriate writing categories. When the existing binder becomes full, simply introduce a new one. Keep your distinctive collection of published works on display at all times.

Andrea Lau
Doyle-Ryder Elementary
Flint, MI

Thematic Presentations

Notably conclude your thematic studies with theme-related literary presentations. Invite a neighboring classroom, your youngsters' families and friends, or other desired guests to attend each presentation. If appropriate, encourage students to dress in theme-related attire. You might also consider serving theme-related refreshments. Ask students to share their favorite theme-related memoirs such as poems, stories, and reports. Or have students write and perform a theme-related play for their guests. The possibilities are endless!

Leslee McWhirter—Gr. 1
Mendel Elementary
Houston, TX

Spelling

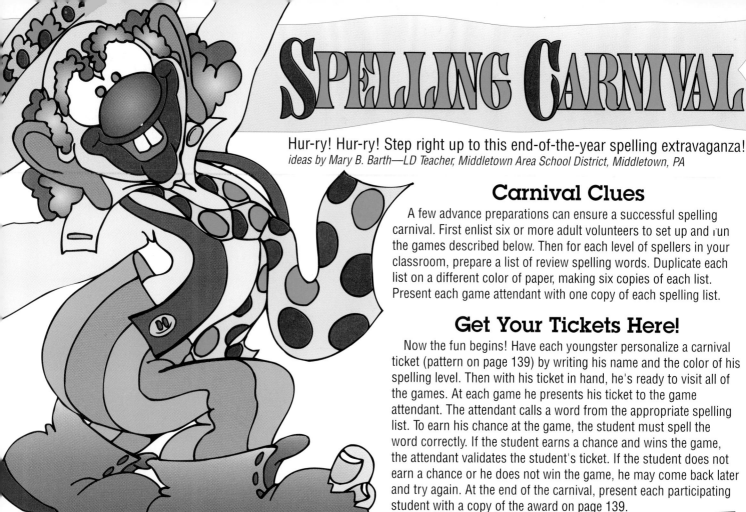

SPELLING CARNIVAL

Hur-ry! Hur-ry! Step right up to this end-of-the-year spelling extravaganza!
ideas by Mary B. Barth—LD Teacher, Middletown Area School District, Middletown, PA

Carnival Clues

A few advance preparations can ensure a successful spelling carnival. First enlist six or more adult volunteers to set up and run the games described below. Then for each level of spellers in your classroom, prepare a list of review spelling words. Duplicate each list on a different color of paper, making six copies of each list. Present each game attendant with one copy of each spelling list.

Get Your Tickets Here!

Now the fun begins! Have each youngster personalize a carnival ticket (pattern on page 139) by writing his name and the color of his spelling level. Then with his ticket in hand, he's ready to visit all of the games. At each game he presents his ticket to the game attendant. The attendant calls a word from the appropriate spelling list. To earn his chance at the game, the student must spell the word correctly. If the student earns a chance and wins the game, the attendant validates the student's ticket. If the student does not earn a chance or he does not win the game, he may come back later and try again. At the end of the carnival, present each participating student with a copy of the award on page 139.

PAM CRANE

CARNIVAL GAMES

Bowl-A-Word

Six empty, two-liter soda bottles and a large rubber ball are needed for this bowling game. On the floor, arrange the soda bottles in a triangle shape. The object is to knock over all six bottles with one roll of the ball. To earn a chance, a student must correctly spell a word.

Spelling Hoopla

A Hula-Hoop® and a toy airplane (made from balsa wood or Styrofoam®) are needed for this game. Suspend the Hula-Hoop® from the ceiling. The object is to fly the toy plane through the Hula-Hoop®. To earn a chance, a student must correctly spell a word.

Spell And Pop

For this game, label one paper strip per student with a spelling prize such as "a special sticker." Place each strip in a balloon; then inflate the balloon. The object is to pop a balloon (by sitting on it) and win the prize listed inside. To earn a chance, a student must correctly spell a word.

Beanbag Toss

Three shoeboxes and six beanbags are needed for this game. Arrange the shoeboxes as desired. The object is to toss two beanbags into each shoebox. To earn a chance, a student must correctly spell a word.

Jump And Spell

A jump rope and a word card labeled "carnival" are needed for this game. The object is to spell the word *carnival* while jumping rope—calling one letter after each jump! To earn a chance, a student must correctly spell a word.

Fishy Fun

For this event, label several fish cutouts with spelling fortunes such as "You're hooked on spelling!" and "You'll tackle any spelling word!" Attach a paper clip to the mouth of each cutout. Place the cutouts on a length of blue bulletin-board paper cut into the shape of a pond. Next make a fishing pole by attaching one end of a length of twine to a dowel and the other end to a magnet. The object is to "catch" a spelling fortune. To earn a chance, a student must correctly spell a word.

SPELLING CARNIVAL
ADMIT ☆ ONE

Bowl-A-Word	Spelling Hoopla	Spell And Pop
Beanbag Toss	Jump And Spell	Fishy Fun

Name _____   Color _____

©1998 The Education Center, Inc. • *The Best Of* THE MAILBOX® *Language Arts* • *Primary* • TEC1459

OUTSTANDING SPELLING
stole the show!

_____'s

©1998 The Education Center, Inc. • *The Best Of* THE MAILBOX® *Language Arts* • *Primary* • TEC1459

Note To Teacher: Use the carnival ticket and spelling award with the ideas on page 138.

Going BANANAS Over Spelling

Inspire your students to become better spellers with this "a-peel-ing" collection of classroom-proven activities, games, and motivational tips!

Shapely Tests

How can you make spelling tests more student-friendly? Try providing seasonally shaped test papers! For each month of the school year, select a simple seasonal shape. Program the shape with numbered lines to accommodate your weekly word list; then duplicate a class set for each spelling test planned that month. After administering a test, provide time for students to color and cut out their seasonal shapes. (Caution students to not color over their spelling words.) Then collect and grade the test papers. When the graded tests are returned, invite interested students to post their shapely spelling at a seasonal display.

*Lisa A. Barone-Papa—Gr. 2
Marquis de Lafayette School #6
Elizabeth, NJ*

Name —————
Spelling Test

1. ———   6. ———
2. ———   7. ———
3. ———   8. ———
4. ———   9. ———
5. ———   10. ———

You're top banana!

More Than Spelling

This spelling review zeros in on the meanings of the weekly words. Write each spelling word on the chalkboard and ask students to number their papers accordingly. In random order, state a clue for each spelling word. After each clue is given, a student copies the appropriate spelling word on his paper. Now that's a meaningful spelling activity!

*Tina McSoley—Gr. 2, Warfield Elementary
Indiantown, FL*

A Personalized Approach

Incorporating your youngsters' names into weekly spelling activities is a great way to heighten student interest. During your final spelling test, insert the name of the Student Of The Week into your sample sentences. Also include student names in your weekly sentence dictation. Students will enjoy hearing the names, and will quickly learn to spell them, too!

*Margie Rusnak—Gr. 3, St. Bernadette School
Milwaukee, WI*

Picture-Perfect Spelling

Puzzling for a different way to introduce spelling words? Divide a simple shape into puzzle pieces—one piece per spelling word. Program the resulting puzzle and duplicate a class set. Give each student a zippered plastic bag and a copy of the puzzle. Instruct each student to cut out the large shape, then cut apart and store his puzzle pieces in the plastic bag. During the week have students practice their spelling words with partners. When a student feels he has mastered a spelling word, he underlines the word on his corresponding puzzle piece. His goal for the week is to underline each spelling word. After the final spelling test has been given, have each student assemble and glue his puzzle pieces on a 9" x 12" sheet of construction paper. The weekly spelling words have now become works of art!

Suzanne Albaugh—Gr. 2, Wintersville Elementary, Wintersville, OH

Heads Up, Spell Up!

A spelling twist makes this version of the popular game Seven Up a class favorite. Select seven student helpers to stand at the front of the room, facing their classmates. Announce, "Heads down, thumbs up!" to indicate that each seated player is to lay her head on her desktop, close her eyes, and extend one thumb. Each student helper quietly tags a seated player by gently pressing down the student's raised thumb. When the student helpers are back in position, announce, "Heads up, spell up!" The players who were tagged stand up. In turn give each standing player a spelling word. If a player correctly spells her word, she has two guesses to identify the helper who tagged her. If she misspells the word, she has one guess. If a player identifies the helper who tagged her, the two students trade places. A new round begins after each standing player has taken her turn. Monitor play to be sure that all students have several spelling opportunities.

Lori DeLaurie—Gr. 2, Heritage Lakes School, Carol Stream, IL

Sit 'n' Spell

This partner activity proves that two heads are better than one! Write the spelling word list on the chalkboard. Have the students sit in two lines facing one another, so that only one line of students can view the word list. Next have the students identify their spelling partners—the classmates who are sitting directly across from them. The students who can see the chalkboard are the "callers," and their partners are the "spellers." A caller reads a spelling word aloud and listens carefully as his partner spells the word for him. If a correct spelling is given, he reads aloud the next word on the list. If an incorrect spelling is given, the caller repeats the word and the two partners spell it together. After a predetermined amount of time, the partners change positions and the activity is repeated. Seeing, saying, and spelling the weekly words is a great way to prepare for an end-of-the-week spelling test!

April Johnson—Gr. 3
Morningside Elementary
Perry, GA

Spelling Bee Jubilee

This unique variation of the traditional spelling bee allows for all players to participate throughout the game! Have students stand side by side in a single line. Call out a spelling word. The first student in line announces the first letter of the called word. The next student in line announces the second letter of the word, and so on until the entire word has been spelled. If a student gives an incorrect letter, he moves to the end of the line, but he still continues to play in the game. When the first word has been correctly spelled, call another spelling word. When the last student in the line calls a letter, play continues at the beginning of the line. Continue in this manner until each spelling word has been spelled at least one time. With no winners or losers, students are eager to participate in this spelling review!

Mary Ann Taxis—Grs. K–5 Reading Specialist
Dalmatia Elementary
Dalmatia, PA

Weekend Challenge

Each Friday give your students a preview of the following week's spelling words. To do this, introduce the spelling rule, pattern, or sound that will be featured. Then challenge each child to look during the weekend for words that contain the featured rule, pattern, or sound. On Monday morning set aside time for students to share their resulting word lists. Then introduce the spelling words for the week. If desired, award extra credit or free spelling passes to students who completed the weekend activity.

Brandi Lampl
W. A. Fountain Elementary
Forest Park, GA

Dartboard Spelling

Ready, aim, spell! This large-group game is right on target when it comes to reinforcing spelling *and* math skills. Display a dartboard and use masking tape to indicate a dart-throwing line. You will also need two safety darts. Group the students into two teams. Alternating between the teams, announce a spelling word to one team member. If the player correctly spells the word, he earns two dart throws. His scores are then added and recorded on the chalkboard under the name of his team. If the player misspells the word, the word is given to a member of the opposing team. If this player responds correctly, he earns two dart throws. If he misspells the word, it is repeated to a different member of the first team, and so on until the word is spelled correctly; then a different word is called. Play continues until all the spelling words for the week have been spelled correctly. Then enlist your students' help in calculating the total score for each team. That's "sum" spelling review!

Kimberlee Zimmerman—Gr. 2, Coal City Elementary School, Coal City, IL

An Instant Review

Reinforce spelling skills and initial consonants with this small-group activity. Each child in the group needs a sheet of paper and a pencil. Announce an initial consonant; then invert an egg timer. Each student writes words on his paper that begin with the designated consonant. His goal is to write as many correctly spelled words as he can. When time runs out, each student counts the words in his list and writes the total near the top of his paper. Quickly review each child's list to determine the number of correctly spelled words; then use a calculator to determine his percentage of correctly spelled words. Have the students record their personal percentages on individual bar graphs. Repeat the activity each week, using a different initial consonant each time. No doubt your youngsters will be spellbound over this unique spelling challenge!

Eleanor Beson—Grs. K–6 Special Education
Ballard Elementary School
South Glens Falls, NY

Poetic Spelling

For a fresh approach to spelling, try putting a poetic spin on your weekly word list. At the beginning of the week, distribute student copies of a poem that reflects a classroom theme, a topic of study, or the current season. As a class, read and discuss the poem; then enlist your students' help in choosing words from the poem for your weekly spelling list. Students are especially motivated to learn to spell the words since they helped choose them. As an added bonus, the youngsters quickly become well versed in a variety of poetry!

Tina McSoley—Gr. 2
Warfield Elementary
Indiantown, FL

SPELLING STARS

Week 1	✦ ✦ ✦ ✦ ✦
Week 2	✦ ✦ ✦
Week 3	✦ ✦ ✦
Week 4	✦ ✦ ✦ ✦
Week 5	
Week 6	

Spelling Stars

Motivate students to prepare for their weekly spelling tests with this star-studded bulletin board. Create a display like the one shown that features each week in the grading period. Each week present a personalized star cutout to every student who earns a perfect score on the weekly spelling test. Then help the star-studded spellers attach their stars to the display. (If desired, hold the final test on Thursday; then on Friday retest those students who would like a second chance at earning a perfect test score.) Throughout the grading period, use the resulting star graph to reinforce a variety of math concepts. At the end of the quarter, hold a popcorn party in honor of your star-studded spellers.

Brooke Swanson—Gr. 2, Inwood Elementary, Houston, TX

Weekly Spelling Chart

A color-coded spelling chart is a great teaching tool. To make a chart, use colorful markers to write the weekly word list on extra large chart paper. Color-code the letters so that the featured spelling rule is made more obvious. Near the bottom of the paper, write "The spelling rule for the week is" and allow room for the sentence to be completed. Post the chart in a prominent classroom location. After the spelling words have been introduced, ask your students to *teach you* the spelling rule of the week. When the students have agreed upon an accurate rule, write it on the chart. Then, during the week, incorporate the chart into a variety of spelling-related activities.

Allyson Birnberg—Gr. 3
Westmoreland Elementary School
Fairlawn, NJ

Spelling

church	chain
cheese	beach
munch	reach
bunch	search
crunch	catch
batch	check
notch	chill

The rule of the week is...

On The Lookout

Encourage students to look for current and previous spelling words in their daily readings. For easy management, give each child a blank journal. When a student identifies a spelling word, he writes the word in his spelling journal, then briefly describes how the word was used and where it was found. Each week, initial the most recent entry in each child's journal. If desired, present small treats or special privileges to students for their efforts. Finding spelling words in a variety of contexts reinforces the meanings of the words and helps students better understand the importance of spelling in everyday life. Who knows? Your students' weekly spelling scores might even improve!

adapted from an idea by Waydean Waller—Gr. 3
Dunbar Elementary School, Texarkana, TX

Jump And Spell

This jump-rope spelling review is sure to receive rave student reviews! In the school gym or on the school playground, display a list of the weekly spelling words. Select two rope turners. As they practice turning a long jump rope, have the remaining students line up a few feet from the turning rope. To begin, call a spelling word. The first player in line runs in. Each time she jumps, she calls out a letter until she has spelled the called word. Encourage the rest of the class to spell the word along with the rope jumper. Then the rope jumper runs out (to the opposite side) and walks around to the back of the line. Continue in this manner until each student, including the rope turners, has had one or more chances to jump and spell. Students will love jumping their way to spelling success!

Betty Kobes—Gr. 1
West Hancock Elementary School
Kanawha, IA

Spelling Bookmark
1.
2.
3.
4.
5.
6.
7.
8.
9.
10.

Spelling Bookmarks

These durable spelling lists can double as bookmarks! Duplicate and cut apart a supply of programmable construction-paper bookmarks like the one shown. Each week distribute a class set of bookmarks. Ask each student to carefully copy the spelling words for the week on his bookmark. Next pair the students so that each child can verify that his partner has copied the spelling words correctly. Encourage students to place the bookmarks in the books they are reading. Each time they have a few minutes to read, they will be reminded to study their spelling words, too.

Lana Stewart—Gr. 1 Chapter I, Wills Point Primary, Wills Point, TX

"Spell-O-Rama"

This review game reinforces the weekly spelling list letter by letter. In advance write the letters of each spelling word on individual cards. Prop a pocket chart (or something similar) in the chalkboard tray and position three player chairs facing the chart. To play, group students into three teams and ask one member from each team to sit in a player chair. Display one set of letter cards facedown in the pocket chart. To begin, one player indicates which card he would like to have turned over by specifying the ordinal position of the card. This player has one guess to identify the word. If he correctly identifies the word, he earns three points for his team. If he can also correctly spell the word, he earns five more team points. When the first player misses, the second player indicates which card he would like to have turned over. The round of play continues until the spelling word has been correctly identified and spelled. Then three different team members sit in the player chairs. Continue the game until each child has been a player one or more times. The team with the most points at the end of game time wins.

Tammi Romenesko—Gr. 1, Central Elementary, Winchester, KY

Tactile Spelling

Students get a real feel for spelling at this center! Partially fill a shallow box with sand, flour, or cornmeal. Place the box and the weekly spelling list at a center. A student reads a word from the spelling list and uses his fingertip to write the word in the box. After he checks his spelling against the provided word list, he uses his hand to smooth out the writing surface; then he repeats the activity using a different spelling word. You can bet that students will be eager to get their hands on this spelling center!

Elysa Cohen—Gr. 3, American International School, Kfar Shmaryahu, Israel

Magnetic Spelling

Make spelling practice more "attractive" with magnetic alphabet letters! For an individual or partner activity, place two metal cookie sheets, a supply of magnetic letters, and a word list at a center. Each student uses the magnetic letters to spell individual words from the list. If two students are working together, they can trade cookie sheets and check each other's spelling. For a whole-group activity, place a container of the letters near your overhead projector and have individual students arrange the letters on the overhead to spell designated words. Have the rest of the class review the projected spellings for accuracy. These nifty alternatives to pencil-and-paper drills are sure to attract student interest!

Sue Connolly—Gr. 2, St. Michael's School, Ridge, MD

BARRY SLATE

Spelling Pays Off

Cash in on this "cents-ible" approach to spelling! Display a poster that shows each alphabet letter and an assigned monetary amount. (See the illustration.) Each week challenge students to find the cash value of each word on their spelling lists. Extend the lesson by using the resulting values in a variety of other activities. For example, have students identify the words that have the highest, the lowest, and the same values. Or have students arrange the words in monetary order as well as alphabetical order. Students are sure to profit from these no-risk spelling activities.

Kim Clasquin—Gr. 1, St. Paul Catholic School, Highland, IL

Money Code

a = 1¢	j = 10¢	s = 1¢
b = 2¢	k = 5¢	t = 2¢
c = 5¢	l = 10¢	u = 5¢
d = 1¢	m = 5¢	v = 1¢
e = 2¢	n = 10¢	w = 2¢
f = 5¢	o = 5¢	x = 5¢
g = 1¢	p = 10¢	y = 1¢
h = 2¢	q = 5¢	z = 2¢
i = 5¢	r = 10¢	

Spelling Grids

Review spelling and map coordinate skills with this kid-pleasing activity! Write the weekly spelling words on a copy of a blank grid; then fill in the remaining boxes with miscellaneous letters. Duplicate and distribute student copies of the programmed grid. Challenge each child to find and circle each spelling word from the weekly list. After the student has found the words, he writes each word on another sheet of paper along with the coordinates of each of its letters. Before long students will be begging to create their own spelling grids! To do this, give each child a copy of a blank grid to program as described above. Then have each student trade grids with a partner to complete the second part of the activity. When the student partners are done, they exchange papers and check each other's work. This activity will quickly become a class favorite!

Sr. Kathleen Leary—Gr. 1, St. Augustine School, Andover, MA

	A	B	C	D	E	F	G	H
12	M	A	Z	B	L	E	P	R
11	s	p	e	l	l	a	i	b
10	c	d	e	w	f	g	h	t
9	u	i	j	k	i	l	m	n
8	r	s	p	m	a	t	h	o
7	s	t	u	m	v	w	h	y
6	c	o	m	e	a	f	h	j
5	g	e	d	c	h	e	a	r
4	l	a	y	o	u	b	r	k
3	m	o	k	e	a	i	e	o
2	o	j	u	m	p	n	p	r
1	j	m	o	e	s	t	a	l

1. come   A6, B6, C6, D6
2. with   D10, E9, F8, G7
3. are   G5, G4, G3
4. it   G11, H10
5. spell   A11, B11, C11, D11, E11

"Spelling-Go-Round"

This spelling game is definitely a step in the right direction! Write the spelling words for the week on individual index cards, repeating the list as needed to create a class set of cards. Tape one card on each student's desktop. Also have each child tape a duplicated spelling list to a sheet of writing paper. To begin play, each child copies the word from her desktop onto her paper and circles the same word on her duplicated spelling list. Then, on your command, each student moves to the next desk along a predetermined route and repeats the activity. Continue in this manner. When a student has circled all the words on her duplicated list at least one time, she calls out "Spelling-Go-Round!" and wins the game. Typically more than one student wins at a time. At the end of game time, collect the cards for later use. For easy storage and organization, use a different color of card (or marker) for each set of spelling cards. The cards can be used again and again and again!

Lisa Buchholz—Gr. 1

Real Or Make-Believe

Reinforce the concepts of real and make-believe with this spelling activity. Ask each student to label one side of a sheet of writing paper "Real" and the opposite side "Make-Believe." As a class, brainstorm several real sentences and several make-believe sentences. Then challenge each child to write three sentences on each side of her paper, using as many of her spelling words as possible. After the sentences have been written, ask each student to reread her work and underline each spelling word she used. If time allows, invite students to illustrate one sentence on each side of their papers.

Lisa Buchholz—Gr. 1, Ben Franklin School
Glen Ellyn, IL

Real-Life Spelling

To reinforce how important spelling is in daily life, try this real-life approach! At the beginning of the week, use a food product such as oatmeal cookies to create your weekly spelling list. If the product has a wrapper, have the students examine it and discuss the spellings of the various words. Or simply use the name of the product. For example, lead a discussion on compound words using *oatmeal* as a springboard. Or have students brainstorm words with the hard sound of *c* or the *oo* sound found in *cookies*. As the students contribute to the discussion, form a list of spelling words from their responses. Then give each child a taste of the featured product. Spelling becomes much more meaningful to students when they understand how it applies to their daily lives. And it's very tasty, too!

Judy Wetzel—Gr. 2
Woodburn School, Oakton, VA

145

Staying In Touch

Put your students in touch with their weekly spelling words! Cut aluminum window screening into 6" x 8" rectangles; then use masking or duct tape to wrap the perimeter of each screen. Place the screens at a spelling center. Each student uses a marker to copy her spelling words on individual word cards. Then, at the center, a student positions each card atop a screen and uses a crayon to trace over the letters of the spelling word. Have each student store her completed set of word cards in a resealable plastic bag. Encourage each student to say the letters of each word as she simultaneously traces them with her fingertip. This kinesthetic learning process gives students a good feel for their weekly spelling words.

Ellen Sue Severson—Grs. 1–6 Resource Teacher
Ballard West School
Slater, IA

I believe the letter is **E** if I'm not mistaken.

fish

...might...

Desktop Review

For an instant spelling review, have each student sit on his desktop. Announce a spelling word. The first player states the first letter of the word. The second player states the second letter of the word, and so on (along an established route of play) until the word has been spelled. If a student states an incorrect letter, he moves to his chair and the next player in route tries to supply the correct letter. A player who is seated in his chair continues to play, and may return to his desktop once he supplies a correct letter. Students think this spelling review is a real winner, and you will, too!

Diane Benner—Gr. 2
Dover Elementary
Dover, PA

Spelling Stories

Students will give this cooperative group approach to spelling practice a thumbs-up! Have each group work together to create a story that contains a predetermined number of words from the weekly spelling list. Once a group completes its story, have the group members practice reading it aloud in preparation for a class presentation. For added fun, have each group agree upon a signal they will use each time a spelling word is read. After each group has presented its story, bind the stories of the week between construction-paper covers and place the book in your classroom library. These weekly publications will be at the top of your students' reading list!

Lisa Buchholz—Gr. 1
Ben Franklin School
Glen Ellyn, IL

Word Of The Day

This daily schoolwide spelling activity is also a great vocabulary builder. Each morning every teacher in the school displays and introduces a designated word of the day and its definition. Throughout the day the word is incorporated into daily activities as much as possible. The school principal even incorporates the word of the day into his morning announcement. Later in the day, the principal circulates around the school with a handful of Word-Of-The-Day certificates. If a student can spell and define the word of the day when asked, the principal presents the student with a certificate. In some classes, the words of the day become the bonus words for the weekly spelling test. It's a daily spelling plan that really works!

Margaret-Ann Rhem—Gr. 3, Western Branch Intermediate
Chesapeake, VA

Spell It!

Reinforce listening skills and provide spelling practice with this bingo-type game. Write the letters of each spelling word on individual construction-paper cards; then place the programmed cards in a container. Each student chooses three words from the weekly spelling list and writes them on his paper. Randomly draw and call out letters from the container. When a child hears a letter that is in one of his words, he crosses out the letter on his card (one time only). The first player to have crossed out each letter in all three of his spelling words stands and declares, "Three-word bingo!" He then reads and spells each word as the caller confirms the called letters. The declared winner of the first game becomes the caller for the second game. To prepare a new game card, each student writes another set of three spelling words on his paper. Students will be begging to play this spelling game each week!

Gina Naseef—Gr. 2, SS Clement-Irenaeus, Philadelphia, PA

Refrigerator Review

Increase your students' spelling-test scores with this unique approach to spelling practice. Each week have students copy their weekly spelling words onto a duplicated form titled "Refrigerator Review." Ask each student to carry his list home and attach it to the family refrigerator. Now each time a family member opens the refrigerator door, the weekly word list will be in plain sight. You can count on the student seeing the list more often in this popular location, and other family members will be tempted to quiz the youngster on his spelling words, too.

Leslie Martinez—Gr. 3, Pine Haven Elementary, Bauxite, AR

Bounce Pass

Students will have a ball playing this outdoor spelling drill. Use chalk to indicate a large X on a blacktop surface. Then draw two parallel lines—on opposite sides of and equal distances from the X. Divide the class into two groups. Have each group stand on opposite sides of the X—perpendicular to the drawn lines. Designate a chalk line for each group. To begin play, the first student in each line stands behind the chalk line so that he is facing a spelling partner from the other group. Hand one player a playground ball; then announce a spelling word. The student holding the ball calls the first letter of the spelling word, then he bounce-passes the ball to his partner. (Suggest that a student try to bounce the ball on the X for an accurate bounce pass.) The second player catches the ball, announces the second letter in the word, and bounce-passes the ball back. Play continues in this manner until the word is spelled. Then each player moves to the end of his group's line and the next two students step up to play. If a player calls an incorrect letter, his turn is over and the next player on his team takes his place. The round of play begins again. Continue play for as long as desired.

Darlene Weir—Gr. 2, South Elementary School, Mt. Carmel, IL

What's My Word?

To play this spelling game, have your students sit in a large circle. Choose one player to be It. As this student moves to the center of the circle, attach to the back of her clothing a large sticky note that you have labeled with a spelling word. Instruct this student to slowly turn around in the center of the circle so that all seated players can read the spelling word she is wearing. The standing player (It) then asks each of three different seated students for a clue about the spelling word on her back. After the third clue, It states and spells her guess. If she identifies and correctly spells the word, she selects the next player to be It. If she makes an incorrect guess or a spelling error, she continues to gather clues from her classmates until she is successful. Then she selects the next person to be It. Play continues until all the spelling words have been identified and spelled at least once and every child has taken a turn.

Laurie Beth Schwartz—Substitute Teacher
Manlius Pebble Hill School, Dewitt, NY

Everyone's A Winner!

Bedazzle your youngsters with this team approach to the traditional spelling bee. Write a spelling-related sentence on the chalkboard like "I wonder if George Washington knew how to spell 'Mississippi'?" Then line up the students and let the spelling bee begin. If a student correctly spells the word he is given, he erases one letter (or punctuation mark) from the posted sentence. If a student misspells the word he is given, the word is given to the next player in line. When the entire sentence is erased, the spelling bee is over and everyone is still standing! If desired, reward the winners (the entire class) with a special treat or privilege for their spelling efforts. Now that's a spelling bee worth buzzing about!

Miriam Gettinger
South Bend Hebrew Day School, Mishawaka, IN

Team Spell

Group students into two teams to play this fast-paced spelling game. Have each team stand in a straight line that is parallel to and faces the line formed by the opposing team. Ask the first student in each line to step forward. These two students become the first-round players. To begin play, announce a spelling word. The first player to correctly state the number of letters in the called word wins the chance to spell the word. If he spells the word correctly, he earns a point for his team. If the player misspells the word, his opponent respells it. The round is over when the word is spelled correctly. Continue play in this manner until each student has participated in one or more rounds of play. The team with the most points at the end of game time wins.

Stacy Barrett Stuttard, Allegheny 1 Elementary, Duncansville, PA

A One-Of-A-Kind Review

If your students have individualized spelling lists, this review is a perfect choice! It's also a great way to review spelling words from the past grading period—or even the past school year! Write the letters of the alphabet on small construction-paper squares and place the resulting alphabet cards in a container. To play, each child needs a spelling list that is different from each of his classmates' lists and a pencil. (Some of the words on the spelling lists may be shared, but no two lists should be identical.) Randomly draw and call out the letters from the container. A student crosses out each example of the called letter on his list. When a student has crossed out all the letters in a particular word, he raises his hand—and when called upon, he reads and spells aloud the word for his classmates. The game is over when all the alphabet letters have been called—which also means that each student should have read and spelled aloud each word on his list. What a review!

Robert F. Staten—Special Education Teacher
Sandia Park, NM

Name _____

Spelling Is Special

Write your spelling words on the lines.
Color a flower each day you study your words.

1. _____
2. _____
3. _____
4. _____
5. _____

6. _____
7. _____
8. _____
9. _____
10. _____

11. _____
12. _____
13. _____
14. _____
15. _____

Monday

Tuesday

Wednesday

Thursday

Friday

Note To Teacher: Use this open reproducible as desired.

_____

has

"bee-dazzled"

us

with

perfect spelling!

Outstanding!

©1998 The Education Center, Inc.

Buzz! Buzz! Buzz!

_____'s

spelling success
sweetened our day!

©1998 The Education Center, Inc.

Perfect Spelling!

Now, that's something to
buzz about!

©1998 The Education Center, Inc.

Busy As A Bee!

_____'s

spelling
is buzzing
with improvement!

©1998 The Education Center, Inc.

Note To Teacher: Duplicate and present awards to students as desired.

Handwriting

Out-Of-This-World
Handwriting Helpers

Propel your youngsters' penmanship skills to extraordinary heights using this stellar collection of motivational tips and activities.

Reach For The Stars
Send students into orbit with these motivational handwriting tips!

Handwriting Hall Of Fame

Recognize outstanding penmanship by inducting samples of student handwriting into your "Handwriting Hall Of Fame." To create a hall-of-fame display like the one shown, mount a plastic page protector (trim off the holes) in the center of a 12" x 18" sheet of construction paper. Decorate the resulting construction-paper border to resemble a fancy frame and attach a paper plaque titled "Honorable Handwriting." Display the prestigious project in a prominent classroom location. Each week, with great fanfare, recognize one student for his outstanding penmanship. As you slide a sample of his best work into the hall-of-fame display, remark on the positive qualities (neatness, correct letter formation, appropriate spacing, etc.) of the student's written work. One week later, remove the youngster's paper and send it home with a special sticker or a hall-of-fame award (see the pattern on page 157). Then induct another young penmanship pro into the Handwriting Hall Of Fame.

Beth Holliday—Gr. 2
J. L. Mudd Elementary
O'Fallon, MO

Handwriting Helper

Reward your students' handwriting efforts by selecting a Handwriting Helper to assist you during daily handwriting practice. To become your Handwriting Helper, a student must consistently exhibit neat and carefully formed handwriting or have recently demonstrated a marked improvement in his handwriting skills. The student who is selected as the helper for the day offers constructive comments, praise, and encouragement to his classmates who are practicing their handwriting. Students will be eager to write their best in hopes of earning the title of Handwriting Helper.

Diane Fortunato—Gr. 2

Snazzy Pencils

Here's a fun and effective way to encourage students to make an extra effort when writing final drafts and special assignments. In a decorated container, place a colorful assortment of new, sharpened pencils. Allow each student to select a pencil from the container before starting on an extra-important handwriting assignment. Students will be inspired to produce their best work when they use these special pencils!

Diane Fortunato—Gr. 2
Carteret School
Bloomfield, NJ

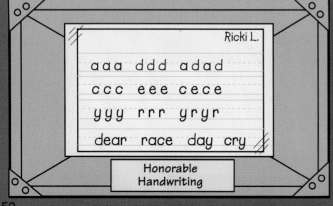

Ricki L.

aaa ddd adad

ccc eee cece

yyy rrr yryr

dear race day cry

Honorable Handwriting

PENCILS

Driven To Success

Have you ever considered that learning to write is similar to learning to drive a car? A student must learn to steer a pencil, stay within the lines, make correct turns, maintain a safe distance between words, and come to a stop at the end of a sentence. Use this analogy to prepare students for handwriting instruction. Then explain that you are their Pencil Driving Instructor and plan to teach them basic writing skills.

When a student feels she has mastered the basic skills, she may apply for a Writer's License by completing a copy of the application form on page 158. Inform students that your evaluation of each applicant will be based on the quality of the penmanship that appears on her application. When a student successfully completes the application, present her with a Writer's License (see the pattern on page 157). After a student has completed the written portion of her license, mount it on construction paper, attach her photo, and laminate the license for durability. Encourage licensed writers to proudly display their writing credentials.

Lori Demlow—Gr. 2, Heritage Lakes School, Carol Stream, IL
Julie A. Hudson—Gr. 2, The Woodlands, TX
Alicia B. Kroll—Gr. 2, Poe International School, Raleigh, NC

North Carolina — Department of Handwriting
Writer's License

Issued to: May Wilson
Room number: 302
School: Bradley
City: Greensboro
Eyes: Brown
Birthdate: 5/8/92

Penmanship Patrol

A Writer's License (see "Driven To Success") is a great way to motivate students to strive for superior penmanship. Explain to new license holders that a licensed writer must consistently demonstrate outstanding writing skills. If a licensed writer shows signs of declining penmanship, issue traffic citations on sticky notes to draw attention to "reckless writing," "failure to stop," "illegal turns," or "excessive speed." The gentle reminders will alert students to potential handwriting hazards.

Julie A. Hudson—Gr. 2

Writing Olympics

Each grading period, challenge students to go for the gold in your Classroom Handwriting Olympics. Create individual performance charts so each student can track his own progress. Then, each time a child earns a star on a handwriting paper, present him with a second star for his performance chart. At the end of the grading period, award construction-paper medals to all participants. Determine your own criteria (based on the number of stars earned) for presenting bronze and silver medals. Bestow the honored gold medal on the student(s) who earned the most stars. If desired, also present a series of congenial awards like "Most Improved Writer," "Most Enthusiastic Writer," and "Most Dedicated Writer."

Alicia B. Kroll—Gr. 2

Chalkboard Critiques

Pique your students' interest in handwriting instruction by inviting them to critique *your* penmanship! Periodically, purposefully include assorted errors when writing a letter, word, or sentence on the chalkboard; then ask students how your handwriting could be improved. Encourage your critics to identify errors in size, spacing, and letter formation. Focusing on such details will help students learn to carefully evaluate their own handwriting.

Lori Demlow—Gr. 2
Kristin McLaughlin—Substitute Teacher, Boyertown, PA

153

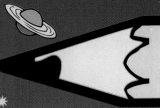

Far-Out Handwriting Activities

Enhance your handwriting instruction with these teacher-tested, student-proven penmanship projects.

Pictorial Penmanship

Here's a picture-perfect way for students to show off their handwriting skills. Give each student a construction-paper booklet of handwriting paper and a set of thematic stickers. (A student needs one sticker for each booklet page.) Instruct each student to personalize the cover of his booklet and attach one sticker to each page. On the chalkboard, write a word that describes one of the students' stickers. Ask the students to find the matching sticker in their booklets and use their best handwriting to copy the corresponding word on the same page. Continue in this manner until each sticker has been labeled. Now, that's picture-perfect handwriting practice!

Jeanette M. Sweet—Substitute Teacher
Newport Beach, CA

Practice With Proverbs

For a variation on traditional handwriting practice, look to proverbs! Model correct letter formation as you write the first part of a proverb on the chalkboard. Some choices are "If at first you don't succeed…" and "Where there's smoke there's...." Have each student copy the phrase on story paper, complete the proverb using his own words, and illustrate his work. If you plan to repeat the activity using several different proverbs, collect and file the students' work in individual student folders. At the end of the grading period (or when appropriate), bind each student's illustrated proverbs between construction-paper covers. The resulting booklets—which will be filled with profound wisdom—will be greatly enjoyed by family members!

Linda Stroik—Gr. 2
Bannach Elementary
Stevens Point, WI

Career Correspondence

This letter-writing activity helps students discover that good handwriting is essential in most careers. To begin ask each student to name a career that intrigues him. Then give the resulting career list to an adult volunteer or your media specialist. Ask for her help in finding the names and addresses of professionals who hold the jobs listed. When the groundwork is done, have each child write a friendly letter asking how writing skills are used in his preferred profession. Be sure each child includes his mailing address or a self-addressed envelope for a speedy reply. Although the job titles vary, most professionals will cite specific examples of how writing skills play a significant role in their careers. Students will love sharing the responses they receive, and they will have a new awareness of the importance of good penmanship in everyday life.

Nancy Sheridan—Multi-Age Grs.1–2
Lines Elementary
Barrington, IL

3-D Handwriting

Here's a fun way to put students in touch with handwriting practice. Use puffy fabric paint to write the alphabet on laminated sentence strips. When they're dry, place the strips in a center for students to touch and trace with their fingers. Students will get a real feel for handwriting practice!

Cathy Barge—Gr. 3, Wiederstein Elementary, Cibolo, TX

Write It Together

If you're looking for a way to keep students interested in handwriting practice, go directly to the source! Each day enlist your students' help in creating a sentence or paragraph for penmanship practice. As you write the student-created material on the overhead or chalkboard, ask your youngsters to assist you with correct spelling, capitalization, and punctuation. You can count on the resulting handwriting assignment to receive a thumbs-up from your youngsters, and you'll have squeezed another teachable moment into your day!

Joan Costello—Grs. K–1
McGinn Elementary School
Scotch Plains, NJ

Palatable Penmanship

For a mouthwatering approach to handwriting, try a recipe center. Place a variety of children's recipe books, a stack of large index cards, a file box, and pencils at a center. A student reads through the recipe books to find a recipe that especially appeals to him. Then, using his neatest handwriting, he copies his chosen recipe on an index card and places the card in the file box. When each student has a recipe card on file, take a class vote to determine the five most delicious-sounding recipes. Then make plans for students to prepare the recipes.

Jennifer L. Morici—Gr. 3
Reeds Road Elementary School
Absecon, NJ

Piggy Popcorn Balls

1 cup corn syrup
9 cups popped corn
1/2 cup sugar
1 6-oz. box of strawberry gelatin

A Weekly Diary

Use this handwriting activity every Friday! Begin by asking students to recall special school-related events from the past week. Write their ideas on the chalkboard in complete sentences. On handwriting paper have each child write her name and the date, then copy three or more of the displayed sentences. Encourage the students to copy the sentences that mean the most to them. Collect their work and file it in individual student folders. At the end of the year, help each child chronologically compile her weekly writings into a booklet. Each student will have firsthand evidence of her penmanship progress, as well as a wonderful keepsake of special memories.

Peg Green—Gr. 2
Trinity Lutheran School
Delray Beach, FL

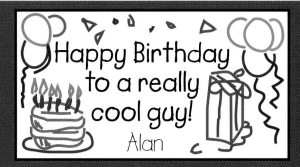

Happy Birthday to a really cool guy!
Alan

Birthday Greetings

How do you incorporate penmanship practice into a birthday celebration? Try this! On a student's birthday, enlist your youngsters' help in creating a desired birthday message; then have each child (with the exception of the birthday child) copy and sign the message in his finest handwriting on a 9" x 12" sheet of white construction paper. Allow time for students to decorate their birthday messages as desired; then compile the messages between construction-paper covers. Label the front cover "Birthday Greetings From _____." If desired, paint a thin coat of diluted glue in each corner of the front cover and sprinkle colorful paper confetti on the glued surfaces. When the glue has dried, shake off the excess confetti. When you're ready to present the booklet of birthday greetings, ask your students to join you in a rousing chorus of a favorite birthday song. Children who celebrate their birthdays during the summer months can receive their birthday booklets at other times of the year.

Jane Walsh—Gr. 1, Brentwood School, Alachua, FL

Riddles For Writing

Since kids love them, riddles are a perfect choice for penmanship practice! Give each student a construction-paper booklet of handwriting paper titled "A Riddle A Day." Have students personalize the covers of their booklets as desired, then store the booklets inside their desks. Every morning write a riddle on the chalkboard for each student to copy in his booklet. Invite students to try to solve the riddle, but ask that they keep their answers a secret until a designated time later that day. When it's time for the riddle answer to be revealed, invite students to share their ideas. Then write the correct riddle answer on the chalkboard for each student to copy. *Why Did The Chicken Cross The Road?* compiled by Joanna Cole and Stephanie Calmenson (Morrow Junior Books, 1994) is an excellent riddle resource.

Lisa Kelley—Gr. 1
James Walker Elementary
Blue Springs, MO

What side of a chicken has the most feathers?

The outside!

Penning Poetic

Acquaint students with the work of several poets by incorporating poetry into your handwriting lessons. At the beginning of each week, display a poem that relates to the season or a current topic of study. Have students copy the poem for handwriting practice. During the week, incorporate the poem into other areas of the curriculum. For example, students can chorally read the poem, find verbs in the poem, or find out something about the poem's author. At the end of the week, invite interested students to recite the poem for their classmates.

Tina Marsh—Gr. 2
Jefferson Parkway School
Newnan, GA

Cursive With A Song

Take a musical approach to penmanship practice by playing a recording of *Dr. Seuss's ABC Book* (Beginner Book & Cassette Library, Random House Books For Young Readers, 1988). As the song begins with "BIG A, little a, what begins with A?," each student writes the named letters on his handwriting paper. Students continue listening and writing as the book proceeds from *A* through *Z*. If the pace of the recording is too fast for your students' handwriting capabilities, read (or sing) the book aloud and adjust your reading (or singing) pace as needed. This is one handwriting activity students will request time and time again!

Carol Morris—Gr. 2, R. A. Doyle Elementary, East Prairie, MO

Alphabetical Review

Plan an alphabetical handwriting review! Each day review the correct uppercase and lowercase formation of a different alphabet letter. Then challenge students to write and illustrate an alliterated animal-related sentence that features the reviewed letter. (For example, "Alfred Anteater ate an apple" or "Zip the zebra zigzagged around the zoo.") Each day collect the students' work and file it in individual student folders. When all the alphabet letters have been reviewed, have each student alphabetically compile his work between construction-paper covers. Provide time for students to enjoy reading their own work and the work of their classmates.

Catherine Lifrieri—Gr. 1, St. Margaret's-McTernan School, Waterbury, CT

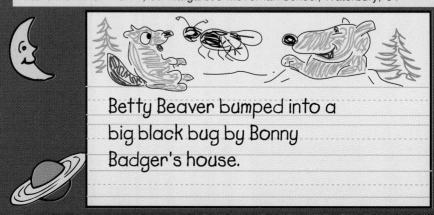

Betty Beaver bumped into a big black bug by Bonny Badger's house.

Department of Handwriting

Writer's License

_____ (state)

Issued to:

Grade:

Room number:

School:

City:

Height:

Eyes:

Birthday:

(signature)

©1998 The Education Center, Inc.

Department of Handwriting

Writer's License

_____ (state)

Issued to:

Grade:

Room number:

School:

City:

Height:

Eyes:

Birthday:

(signature)

©1998 The Education Center, Inc.

On

_____ (date)

the attached handwriting was inducted into the **Handwriting Hall Of Fame**

_____ (official signature)

©1998 The Education Center, Inc.

Use the award with "Handwriting Hall Of Fame" on page 152.

Writer's License Application Form

Complete the following information.
Use your very best handwriting!

Today's date: _____

Your name: _____

Grade level: _____

Teacher's name: _____

Name of school: _____

Color of your eyes: _____

Color of your hair: _____

Your favorite food: _____

On the lines below, write why you think you should be a licensed writer.

_____

_____

_____

_____

Signature Of Applicant:

_____

Note To Teacher: Use with "Driven To Success" on page 153.

Answer Keys

Page 28
1. top
2. strong
3. enemy
4. afraid
5. open
6. big
7. sell
8. day
9. asleep
10. curly
11. back
12. work

Page 29

Page 30
1. sour
2. large
3. cold
4. long
5. thick
6. hard
7. small
8. delicious
9. large
10. thin
11. fast
12. creamy

Page 49

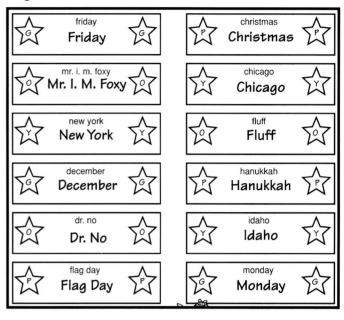

Page 54

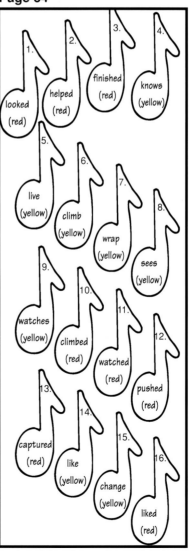

Answer Keys

Page 74

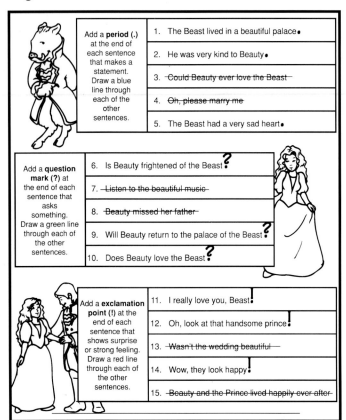

Add a **period (.)** at the end of each sentence that makes a statement. Draw a blue line through each of the other sentences.

1. The Beast lived in a beautiful palace.
2. He was very kind to Beauty.
3. ~~Could Beauty ever love the Beast~~
4. ~~Oh, please marry me~~
5. The Beast had a very sad heart.

Add a **question mark (?)** at the end of each sentence that asks something. Draw a green line through each of the other sentences.

6. Is Beauty frightened of the Beast?
7. ~~Listen to the beautiful music~~
8. ~~Beauty missed her father~~
9. Will Beauty return to the palace of the Beast?
10. Does Beauty love the Beast?

Add a **exclamation point (!)** at the end of each sentence that shows surprise or strong feeling. Draw a red line through each of the other sentences.

11. I really love you, Beast!
12. Oh, look at that handsome prince!
13. ~~Wasn't the wedding beautiful~~
14. Wow, they look happy!
15. ~~Beauty and the Prince lived happily ever after~~

Page 75

1. Three bears lived in a house in the woods.
2. Goldilocks took a walk in the woods.
3. Why did Goldilocks walk into the bears' home?
4. Each of the three bears had a bowl of porridge.
5. Wow, that porridge is hot!
6. Oh no, the chair broke!
7. Should Goldilocks go upstairs?
8. What a huge bed!
9. Goldilocks fell fast asleep in Baby Bear's bed.
10. The three bears came home.
11. Who has been eating my porridge?
12. Who broke Baby Bear's chair?
13. Look who is in my bed!
14. Will the bears ever see Goldilocks again?

Page 79

Asking Sentences

Were all dinosaurs big?
What does dinosaur mean?
How often did dinosaurs eat?
How do we know about dinosaurs?
What did dinosaurs like to eat?
What made dinosaurs die out?

Telling Sentences

Some dinosaurs were little.
It means terrible lizard.
Some dinosaurs ate all day long.
Bones and tracks were found.
Most ate plants.
Maybe it got too cold for them.

(Includes Bonus Box answers)

Page 76

Correct sentences: 2, 4, 5, 8, 10, 12, 13, 15
Incorrect sentences: 1, 3, 6, 7, 9, 11, 14

Page 120

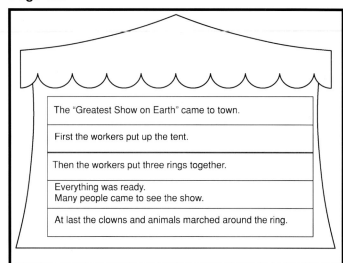

The "Greatest Show on Earth" came to town.

First the workers put up the tent.

Then the workers put three rings together.

Everything was ready.
Many people came to see the show.

At last the clowns and animals marched around the ring.

Page 121

Tubby is the funniest clown in the circus.
yellow
I would like to be a clown someday.
red
Tubby's hair sticks out all over his head.
yellow
JoJo is the saddest clown.
red
Tubby throws pies at the other clowns.
yellow
One time he wore his shoes backward.
yellow
Bubbles is a clown, too.
red
Tubby is a funny guy!
yellow
Now read the yellow stripes to check your answers.